DRIED FLOWERS
FROM THE GARDEN

A PRACTICAL GUIDE TO GROWING, DRYING AND ARRANGING

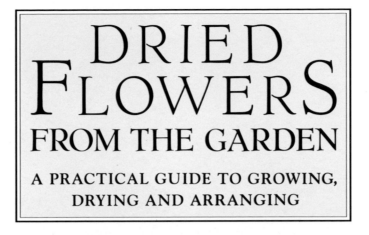

HarperCollins*Publishers*

DRIED FLOWERS

FROM THE GARDEN

A PRACTICAL GUIDE TO GROWING, DRYING AND ARRANGING

MOLLY EPHRAUMS AND JANE IRONSIDE

Acknowledgements

To Roger and Frank, with grateful thanks
for their constant help and encouragement.

The author and the artist would like to thank all those who have assisted them in the creation of this book, with special thanks to the following: Christine Carter; Genevieve Cruikshank; Paulette and Tim Doncaster; Roger Ephraums; Trevor Harrison; Sue and John Holman; Frank Jarvis; Geeta Maude-Roxby and Richard Scott; George Park (of K. Sahin, Zaden BV, Holland); The Royal Botanic Garden, Edinburgh; R. Stennett-Wilson; Alasdair Sutherland; Robin Taylor; Thompson & Morgan; University Botanic Garden, Dundee.

First published in 1992 by
HarperCollins Publishers, London

Text © Molly Ephraums 1992
Colour illustrations © Jane Ironside 1992

Photographs
© Adrian Bloom 1992 (pp. 93, 104)
© Boys Syndication/Jacqui Hurst 1992 (pp. 52, 72, 90, 106)
© Molly Ephraums 1992 (pp. 8, 18, 20, 23, 25, 31, 76, 85, 86, 87, 93, 94, 96, 97, 104, 108)
© Roger Ephraums 1992 (pp. 13, 21)
© Michael Warren 1992 (pp. 64, 77, 102)
© Jacqui Hurst 1992 (all remaining photographs)

Dried flower arrangements and styling: Jane Ironside
Props supplied by: Richard Scott Antiques, 30 High Street, Holt, Norfolk.

Commissioning Editor: Polly Powell
Designer: Caroline Hill
Colour illustrations: Jane Ironside
Line illustrations: Tig Sutton
Index: Dorothy Frame

A CIP catalogue record for this book is available from the British Library

ISBN 0 00 412652 1

Typeset in Concorde
by Phoenix Photosetting, Chatham, Kent
Colour reproduction in Singapore, by Colourscan
Manufactured in Spain, by Graficromo

Contents

INTRODUCTION

This book is the result of a chance meeting some years ago between Jane Ironside and myself. Having seen her beautiful work, I asked Jane to paint two pictures for me, incorporating all the dried flowers that I grew at that time. We met at Jane's house and while she showed me round her garden we discussed the different varieties of dried flowers; the way we grew them; the problems we faced with our northern climate; and the difficulties that wet summers created. We discussed how we had had to learn by trial, error and experience the best way to deal with all these things. While there are many books on arranging dried flowers, neither of us had found one that told us all we needed to know about growing them. We agreed that had one been available it would have saved us a great deal of time and wasted effort.

What was needed, we decided, was a reference book, and we would produce it, giving all the varieties of plants which are suitable for drying. Each plant would be accompanied by botanical illustrations, and all the relevant information on how to grow, support, pick and dry them. Information about each one's hardiness, what pests and diseases could attack them, what conditions they need in order to produce good flowers, and how tall they grow would be provided. All these things we had had to find out for ourselves, and our years of shared experience would be put into the book – this book.

Everyone who loves flowers experiences not only the joy of seeing them bloom, but also the sadness of watching them die, knowing that it will be a year until they are seen again. However, immortelles, or perpetuelles, to give dried flowers their correct name, that are picked in the summer, will still be as bright and as colourful in the winter as on the day they were gathered. Many of them will last for years and can be used over and over again in different arrangements. Immortelles have evolved to withstand hot, dry conditions, and come mainly from the Mediterranean, South Africa, Australia and New Zealand, though some grow in Europe and less temperate areas. Most, but not all, are annuals. Many herbaceous and other plants also dry well.

All the varieties listed here have been tried and tested, and should do well. It is always worth experimenting with new introductions in your garden for then each year will bring new discoveries and surprises. My advice is to try them all, and to experiment with any other varieties that look promising. Obviously, results will depend on where you live,

OPPOSITE: Centaurea macrocephala, Eryngium alpinum, *delphinium*, Linum usitatissimum *and grasses hanging up to dry.*

the quality of your soil, the weather, how sheltered your garden is, and, of course, your skill as a gardener.

Most of the plants described are easy to grow, and quite a few of the annuals tolerate poor soil. I hope that even though you may be growing them for the first time, the information in the following chapters will enable you to achieve satisfactory results at your first attempt. I should warn you, however, that dried flowers are very addictive. Jane and I have been growing them for many years, and at the end of each exhausting season we vow that we shall never do so again; the following spring, however, finds us enthusiastically sowing and planting once more.

Throughout the book I refer to 'growing on a large scale' or 'growing for your own use'. Large scale refers to small businesses, not to commercial growers who have whole fields of dried flowers. My garden measures 36 × 75ft (11 × 23m), and is divided into halves; one side for perennials and the other for annuals, with large or invasive plants in 3ft (1m) beds around the sides. From this garden I grow enough material to supply several shops and many individual customers with bunches of flowers, and small arranged baskets. I can fulfil orders for large arrangements in churches and peoples' homes and have sufficient left for my own use.

Growing for your own use means just that, with perhaps some left over for friends. For such requirements you will need very few plants. Some of the annual flowers make excellent bedding plants, are very floriferous, and are tolerant of crowded conditions.

Tables of Quantities of Seed and Plants required for large and small scale growth are at the end of the book, but you will have a better idea of the amounts you need after your first growing season.

If you are planning to grow plants on a large scale, do bear in mind that you will need to tend your plants and garden for at least six or seven months of the year. If you are sowing in the spring, harvesting will not be finished until the autumn. In the summer, weather permitting, most afternoons will be spent bending over, cutting the flowers. Remember, too, that there is all the attendant work of digging, weeding, lifting and dividing perennials, moving compost in wheelbarrows and all the other jobs that go with any garden. Most dried flowers keep in perfect condition for up to nine months, or longer if they are kept dry and out of bright sunlight, so there may well be flowers to sell all year round.

Molly Ephraums' garden near Arbroath, Scotland.

Despite the work, though, it is healthy and rewarding. Harvesting flowers in the peace of your own garden on a sunny day must be preferable to many other occupations.

Of course, much will depend on the time you can give to the enterprise, and what help you can get, and afford. It may not be difficult finding someone who can dig and weed for you, but helpers who can be trusted to look after seedlings, and are nimble fingered enough to do the picking and wiring may be another matter. Keep all this in mind before embarking on large-scale production; time and experience will guide you to what you can cope with, and then you will be able to expand or contract your growing area accordingly.

If growing for profit, do make initial enquiries to see what local demand is likely to be and what, if any, competition you may have. There is no point in setting up a business only to find that there is another local supplier and shops do not want your flowers. They are bulky, and some are rather fragile, so transporting them any distance has its problems. Time spent in market research is seldom wasted.

Many of the imported dried flowers in the shops are of poor quality and very expensive, so word will almost immediately get around that there is a local supply of good quality flowers, and before long you will probably have more customers than you can cope with. Gift shops and local flower clubs are usually keen to stock them.

GARDENING EQUIPMENT

Sowing Seeds

SEED TRAYS

You will need both full- and half-sized seed trays, and some of the excellent polystyrene sectioned trays that are now available. These allow the seedlings to grow contained in their own section, and they are then popped out with no damage to the roots, such as you get when cutting seedlings out of a standard seed tray. Peat discs that swell when immersed in water are also available. You could also try making your own compost blocks, but the sectioned trays are by far the best and make planting out quick and easy.

If you are growing perennials, you will also need a good stock of pots of various sizes and depths.

SEED PACKETS

Seed firms differ greatly in the quantity of seed provided in their packets. If you think you have bought a packet containing too few seeds, it may be worth writing to the company concerned – you never know, you may receive another packet in its stead.

Pricking out
eryngium seedlings.

LABELS AND PENS

Ensure that the pen you use is water- and lightproof. It is nothing short of a disaster if you cannot tell your helichrysum seedlings from your helipterums because the writing on the label has disappeared. Some people use a crayon or pencil instead of a pen.

Small, white plastic labels are best for marking the seed trays, and wooden sticks for marking rows. Large plastic labels break if you tread on them. A plastic label can be used for pricking out very small seedlings, although a plastic dibber is best for pricking out the average-sized seedling.

SPRAYS AND WATERING CANS

You will need a hand spray for watering the seedlings in their early stages, followed by a small watering can with a fine rose. Big watering cans are very heavy to lift up to staging level, and can swamp the seedlings, so are best kept for use in the cold frame and when the seedlings have been planted out. You will also need a hose with a hand trigger, or a sprinkler, for use in the garden during dry weather.

COMPOST

This is a matter of personal choice, and can be either a soil-based or peat-based soilless compost. Soilless composts made from coconut coir and other materials that do not contain peat are now available. It is always wise to buy a good brand, and not to economize. The cheaper ones can be lumpy and not altogether suitable for sowing small seeds.

Gardening equipment:
1 *Pots;* **2** *Fertilizer;*
3 *Perlite;* **4** *Propagator;*
5 *Hose with fine spray;*
6 *Trowel;* **7** *Soil compactor;* **8** *Cheshunt compound;* **9** *Waterproof pens;* **10** *Plastic labels;*
11 *Seed packets;* **12** *Hand spray;* **13** *Seed trays;*
14 *Temperature gauge.*

Raising Seedlings

PROPAGATORS

Seeds need warmth and moisture to germinate, and the best way to provide these is to put the seed trays in a propagator in which the correct temperature can be maintained and moisture generated. Cuttings, too, root more quickly with heat and humidity.

If you are growing plants on a large scale, you will need a large propagator. There are numerous models available, but they tend to be expensive, and it is much cheaper to make your own. This is easily done using a strong piece of chipboard measuring 3½ft × 2½ft (1.1m × 75cm) for the base, and 12-in (30-cm) wide wooden planks for the sides. The lid should be light and easy to remove, and can be made by stapling strong, clear plastic to wooden battens. The propagator is filled with damp sand in which a thermostatically controlled heating coil is 'sandwiched'. Keep the sand moist at all times to prevent the coil from overheating, and to provide a humid atmosphere.

If you are growing for your own use, there is a good selection of small propagators which take either one full-sized, or two half-sized, seed trays. These are inexpensive and well worth buying, but it is always possible to make do with, for example, the top of a central heating boiler, airing cupboard or windowsill. (Remember: if using a windowsill protect your paintwork with a piece of polythene under the tray.)

THE GREENHOUSE

This is necessary if you are growing more than just one or two trays of seeds. When the seedlings have been pricked out they can stay in the propagator for one or two days, then they should be moved out onto the staging or shelves in the greenhouse.

Lean-to models can have shelves fitted to the rear wall, as this takes in heat during the day and releases it at night, like a storage heater, providing extra warmth for the seedlings. Seed trays on these shelves will need turning each day to prevent the seedlings leaning towards the light. If the shelves are removable they can be taken down later, leaving room there to place tomatoes in the summer, and tall plants that need protection in the winter.

A maximum/minimum thermometer is a great help in the greenhouse, because it enables you to monitor the temperature day and night. If there is electricity in the greenhouse, use a small fan heater worked by a rod thermostat to control the temperature automatically. Heat comes on only when it is needed and warm air is circulated around the house, which helps to discourage mould. There are various other types of heaters available if there is no electricity supply in the greenhouse; your local dealer will advise you on the best model for your type of greenhouse. The temperature needs to be kept at 55–60°F (13–16°C) while the seedlings are small, and gradually reduced to 45–50°F (7–10°C) just prior to putting them out in the cold frame.

It is worth insulating your greenhouse in the winter with plastic 'bubble' sheeting, and leaving it on for added warmth while germinating seeds in early spring. It must be removed as soon as the seedlings are 1in (2.5cm) high, or they will become etiolated. The roof panels

A temperature-controlled propagator is the ideal place to raise your seedlings.

can be left to keep the temperature up at night, but they, too, must be removed as soon as possible.

Always keep a close watch on seedlings. It is amazing how quickly a greenhouse can heat up on a sunny day. Good ventilation is essential, and automatic opening stays on the windows are invaluable. These operate by means of a gel in a cylinder which expands and contracts depending on the amount of heat, and lifts or lowers the window accordingly. They are well worth fitting, but even so you will have to be ready to open and close doors, and to shade the roof and side panels of the greenhouse with green plastic netting if necessary. Another valuable aid is a relation, kind friend or gardener who can competently take over if you are away. Nothing is more distressing than coming home to find that all your precious seedlings have wilted from excessive heat and lack of water.

COLD FRAMES

These are needed for hardening off the seedlings when they leave the greenhouse or, if you do not have a greenhouse, for putting the seed trays in once they are ready to leave the windowsill. A perfectly adequate cold frame can be made by using concrete blocks, bricks, or even strong wooden planks, and an old window. (Builders' yards and skips can often provide these either for free or at minimal cost.) There is a large range of cold frames available, some quite reasonable in price. A cold frame is a worthwhile investment, as it can be used for many flower and vegetable seedlings, and for overwintering tender or young plants that are not ready for planting out until the spring.

HYGIENE

Clean your greenhouse and cold frame in the autumn and, more importantly, in spring before sowing your seeds. In the greenhouse, wash all the glass and the floor with a disinfectant and then fumigate with combined anti-mould, fungicide, and insecticide cone. Thoroughly water any plants in the greenhouse several hours before using such a cone (ensuring you do not wet the leaves), and raise the temperature to the correct level. Do not fumigate in windy weather, as the fumes are very strong. If your greenhouse is attached to your house, have ready some large, wet towels to place against the connecting door to prevent fumes from entering.

Seedlings thrive in the humid conditions of a greenhouse.

A watering can can be used once the seedlings are well established outside.

For larger seeds and for seedlings, use sectioned polystyrene or plastic trays. Equipment for sowing seeds: **1** *Compost;* **2** *Trays;* **3** *Hand spray;* **4** *Soil compactor;* **5** *Plastic labels;* **6** *Waterproof pen;* **7** *Seed packets.*

For the cold frame, wash the glass, rake the gravel or turn over the soil – whichever is used for a base – and, if it has a wooden frame, spray an insecticide around the sides and lid to remove any aphids that may have overwintered there. An organic solution of derris or pyrethrum, sprayed from a pump-action spray, is the best mixture to use.

Remember, too, to wash all your pots and seed trays both before and after use; and stand all bamboos in a bucket of disinfectant to clean the soiled ends, before tying them into bundles and storing for the winter.

All these jobs are important; it is easy to neglect them and to hope that all will be well. You may be lucky, but also you may not, and all your efforts will be wasted. You will bitterly regret your lack of precautions and preparations as you watch your seedlings being attacked by aphids or botrytis. If the worst does happen, and sometimes aphids can appear before you have planted out, you will have to spray with a suitable insecticide, being very careful that the solution is not too strong.

GARDEN TOOLS
You will need, and probably will have already, all the basic gardening tools, such as a wheelbarrow, spade, fork, hoe and rake for preparing your ground, and a small trowel and a line marker for planting out your seedlings. You will also need a small hand fork for weeding, secateurs for cutting down your perennials in the autumn, a watering can, and a hose with a hand trigger.

CULTIVATION

Growing your own plants for drying can be very rewarding. Not only do the plants contribute to the garden, but also in their dried form they add interest to any room.

Annuals from Seed

Instructions for each variety are given in the Plant Directory, but some general information on sowing is perhaps necessary for those of you who are inexperienced. Most seed packets, but not all, have full instructions printed on them, and any good gardening book will provide details, but the following advice may be helpful.

SOWING INDOORS
Fill the seed tray with compost to just below the rim and firm gently with a piece of board. If you have a sink you can use, fill it with water to a depth of 1in

ABOVE: *Herbaceous borders, with stakes to support the taller plants.*
PREVIOUS PAGES 116–117: *The dried flower garden in summer.*

(2.5cm) lower than the top of the tray, then gently lower the tray into the water. Make sure the compost is uniformly moist, but not saturated. Lift out the tray and place it on newspaper until all excess water from the compost has drained out.

If you do not have a suitable sink, put the compost in a bucket and add water. Make sure that it is evenly moist before filling the seed trays. No excess water should come out when you squeeze a handful of the compost. It is much better to moisten the compost in advance; watering the seeds after sowing could either moisten only the top of the compost, or swamp it and perhaps wash away the seeds. Once the seed trays are filled, firm the compost gently with a piece of board.

Carefully sprinkle the seeds on the surface. Cover with a little dry compost, or a mixture of sharp sand and compost. Using a hand spray containing an ammonium carbonate and copper sulphate solution (Cheshunt compound), moisten this covering. Sowing the seeds this way means they will stick to the compost and not be disturbed when you spray them. It is always advisable to water in seedlings with this solution to discourage damping off and mould.

Now place the trays in your propagator, airing cupboard or on top of your central heating boiler. (Check the temperature of these with your thermometer.) If the trays are placed on a windowsill, cover them with glass and newspaper until germination takes place, after which these must be removed. Remember to turn the trays each day if they are on the back shelves of a greenhouse or on a windowsill. Propagators generate a lot of moisture on

the sides and lids, so wipe this off regularly or it will encourage algae and mould to grow on the compost, causing your seedlings to damp off. Also, wipe any glass covering seed trays, to stop excess water dripping onto the compost when you inspect the trays each day for signs of germination.

PRICKING OUT

Prick out the seedlings as soon as you can safely handle them, usually when they have two pairs of leaves. Sooner rather than later is best, as you are less likely to damage the roots. Use a small dibber or a plastic label to ease the seedlings out gently, discarding any that are not perfect, or whose roots are broken. (Do not discard any remaining seedlings as you may need them to replace any that do not 'take'.) Plant them five across and seven down in standard seed trays, or preferably in sectioned polystyrene trays, which have been filled with damp compost. Be careful when moving the sectioned trays for the first week or so, for the compost tends to fall out of the holes at the bottom until the roots are large enough to hold it. A sheet of plastic placed on the staging, under the sectioned trays, will prevent this.

At this stage, it is important to make sure that the temperature does not fall below 55–60°F (13–16°C). Reduce this gradually to 45–50°F (7–10°C) in the last week prior to moving the seedlings out to the cold frame to harden off. You will need to watch your seedlings as they grow, nipping out the tips of any that get too tall, to encourage bushy growth. Tall, weak plants do not produce good blooms; they tend to fall over and are damaged by the rain.

a *Firm and level the compost in your seed trays.*

b *After sowing the seeds, sprinkle them with compost and spray lightly to moisten the covering.*

c *Nip out the tips of any 'leggy' seedlings to encourage bushy growth.*

When the seedlings are well established and are about 3–5in (7.5–12.5cm) tall, you can move them out to the cold frame, being sure to protect them both night and day with green netting, or newspaper, for the first few days. Cold is not the only danger: hot sunny days can scorch and dry out the seedlings, so watch them carefully and shade as necessary. Make sure the shading or night covering is well anchored and cannot blow away. Gradually reduce the amount of night protection by leaving the lids open a little, increasing this until you can remove the lids altogether for the last few nights prior to planting out.

During the day you will need to do the same, depending on the weather. On cold days you should leave the lids open a little; on hot days they should be half or fully open. Continue to feed and water the seedlings, and when all danger of frost has passed, you can plant them out.

FERTILIZER
Compost contains sufficient fertilizer for seedlings for the first four to five weeks. After this they need a very weak foliar feed once a week, until they go out into the cold frame, when they get a full-strength feed weekly. Some plants, such as statice (*Limonium sinuata*), need a lot of potash which should be raked into the soil where they will be planted a few weeks prior to putting them out. All rows of plants (with the exception of *Phalaris canariensis* which does not like it) will need a weekly full-strength foliar feed.

PLANTING OUT
Your ground should have been prepared by digging over the soil in the autumn, or early spring, adding compost if necessary. Now rake the soil to remove any lumps and stones, make sure the surface is level, and remove any weeds. If you are setting the plants in rows, you will need to mark these out with a line marker or piece of string fixed to two pegs. Carefully push out the seedlings from the sectioned trays, or cut them carefully out of seed trays, and make holes deep enough to set the plants in, allowing sufficient room for their roots. Firm the plants in well and water immediately. Try to plant out on a still, overcast day; hot sun will wilt the seedlings. Mid- to late afternoon is best, when it is getting cool. The ideal distances between plants and between rows is given in the Plant Directory.

PROTECTING THE PLANTS
If you are bothered by pigeons or cats, you will need to protect the rows with lines of fine string or wire netting. Children's plastic 'windmills' are excellent bird deterrents, especially the red and blue ones (pigeons hate these colours). Keep the rows weeded, watered and fed, nipping out any heads of plants that are growing too tall and lanky, and with sunshine and warmth you should be starting to pick your flowers by the middle of the summer.

SOWING OUTSIDE
You will sow some seeds directly into the flower beds, others in rows (see the Plant Directory for details). Always follow the instructions on the seed packet. Before sowing, prepare your ground, raking it to a fine tilth as described above, and then draw out a shallow drill. If it is a windy day, it is helpful to water the drills before sowing; some seeds are very light and blow away in the wind,

Bamboos and netting used to support young helichrysums.

20

Cloche can be removed once the plants are 2in (5cm) high. These rows of annuals were set out in early summer.

and you will end up having seedlings where you do not want them. Sow evenly and not too thickly, cover the seeds with a fine layer of soil, firm this down and lightly water the rows again. Do not forget to label the rows. When the seedlings are between 1–2in (2.5–5cm) high, thin them out to the distance recommended on the packet, or in the Plant Directory, and continue to feed, water and weed the rows as described above.

CLOCHE

If the weather is cold, and you cannot delay sowing, invest in some of the excellent floating or expanding cloche that is now available. This is a light sheet of material that allows water and sunlight to permeate through. It not only warms the soil, but retains moisture and gives protection from frost in colder areas. You can cut it into lengths and widths to suit the size of your rows. Hold it down with stones, or battens of wood. The latter make it much easier to lift off the cloche and see what is happening underneath. But there is no need to lift the cloche when watering, as the perforations in the material allow the water to pass through. If you can lay it down a few days prior to sowing it will warm up the soil and speed up germination, giving you a flying start in bad years. Washed after use and stored carefully, it lasts for many years.

Leave expanding cloche on until the plants are about 1–2in (2.5–5cm) high, when you will need to ease it up to allow the seedlings to grow straight. Remove the expanding cloche only when all danger of frost has passed.

Perennials from Seed

Transfer the well-formed seedlings into 3in (7.5cm) pots.

Herbaceous plants can be expensive to buy and are not always easy to find locally. The alternative to searching for a particular plant is to grow it yourself; this is cheaper and, if you are prepared to wait one or two seasons for the plant to mature, much more fun. Few things are more rewarding to keen gardeners than the satisfaction of raising their own perennials, especially if they are hard to find or in short supply. It can be disappointing when orders arrive marked 'Out of Stock' beside particularly desired plants; growing them from seed can save years of waiting and frustration. Members of plant societies can buy seed from them. Their lists often include seed not always easily obtained elsewhere.

The most important factor with perennial seeds is freshness. Also, with many seeds a period of stratification is needed. In their natural state seeds ripen, fall to the ground or are spread by birds and the wind, and lie under or on the surface of the soil through the winter, and are thus subjected to rain and frost. This breaks the seeds' dormancy, and the following spring, with warmth and water, they germinate. To imitate this process you must either buy seeds or gather your own just as the seed pods are opening, and sow them in seed trays, covering them with a layer of sharp sand or grit to prevent the growth of algae. Then leave the seed trays either in a cold frame, in very cold areas, remembering to water them, or outside in a corner of the garden where you will not forget them in the spring.

Once the temperature has risen in the spring (when weeds start to grow is a good sign that the time is right) bring the seed trays into the greenhouse, or put them in your cold frame with the lid closed, and with luck the seeds should germinate. Do not be too impatient. You may leave a tray for several months, and just when you think it's lifeless, up will come the seedlings.

PRICKING OUT

When the seedlings are large enough to handle safely (usually when they are larger than you would normally prick out annuals) ease them out of the compost, being very careful not to damage the roots, which may be quite long. Transfer them to 3in (7.5cm) pots, using a multi-purpose compost with a little added grit or expanded volcanic rock (Perlite) to open up the mixture. Label the pots and place them in the cold frame, or keep them in the greenhouse for a few weeks if the weather is cold. Harden off the plants and stand them in a nursery bed on gravel. If you leave them on soil they may well root into this, and then can be difficult to lift without damage.

Always watch young plants carefully in hot weather, being sure to keep them well watered, and shading them if necessary. Feed them with a little organic fertilizer, or weekly foliar feed.

In mid- to late summer, the plants will be ready to plant out in their permanent positions. Any plants that you consider too small to withstand the winter, move into 4–5in (10–12.5cm) pots and put them back into the cold frame until the following spring, when they can be planted out after all danger of frost has passed. Some may flower in their first year, but most of them will wait until the following summer. With luck you will have more plants than you need, and will therefore be able to give the spares to friends or to charity sales, where they will undoubtedly be snapped up enthusiastically.

PLANTING OUT

When planting out a perennial, dig out a suitably sized hole and work in some well-rotted manure or compost. This is particularly important for varieties such as astilbe, which require soil that will retain moisture. Next, work in a handful of Blood, Fish and Bone, or bonemeal. These are slow-acting and will provide the necessary food to help the plant get established during its first year. They are preferable to inorganic fertilizers which can sometimes encourage too rapid growth. Firm the plant in well, then water and label it.

MULCHES

All perennials like an annual mulch of well-rotted manure or compost in spring, but if this is not available you can use damp peat, or preferably one of the tree bark mulches now on the market, which come in varying grades from fine to coarse. These will help to reduce evaporation of moisture from the soil surface in dry weather, and suppress weeds. If the plants are in a border, watch to see that neighbouring plants do not encroach or shade them while they are still young. Use herbaceous supports if necessary.

In the autumn or early winter, when all the foliage on your perennial plants has died down, cut this off; it can be added to your compost heap if it is not too woody. Clean all the flower beds or borders of weeds, and then lightly fork over the soil.

THE COMPOST HEAP

The compost heap is a most important feature of all gardens, and is the cheapest and best way to obtain your own organic humus and fertilizer. It is the ideal way of turning garden and kitchen waste into the best possible soil enricher. It is very

Centaurea macrocephala *in front of* Echinops sphaerocephalus. *Perennials like an annual mulch of well-rotted manure or compost in the spring.*

easy to make your own container, using four strong posts and planks; ready-made versions are expensive and often too small. Soft weeds that have not set seed, annual plants when they are lifted in the autumn, some grass clippings, vegetable and fruit waste, and the leaves stripped off the stems of your dried flowers when you are bunching them can all be put into a compost heap.

Remember not to put in any weed with a long tap root, such as dock or dandelion and, most important of all, bindweed or couch grass. From one small piece, these pernicious weeds will infiltrate your compost heap and multiply; when the compost is spread on your flower beds and borders they will make your life a misery. Equally, never put cooked food on the compost heap, as this will smell, and encourage raids by rats and mice.

Well-rotted compost dug into your annual flower beds in the autumn is recommended, if not every year, at least once every two or three years. Annual dried flowers are very tolerant of poor soil, but there is a limit to how long even they can flourish in worked out beds.

Some of the items you may need for staking tall plants. There is now a wide range of herbaceous supports available from garden centres and by mail order.

seeds to allow for seasonal variations in germination and any disasters that may occur. Advice on the number of seed packets you will need is given in the Appendices at the end of the book.

ROTATING CROPS
Always rotate your crops, like a farmer. Keep a chart each year of where you plant each variety, and try to put a different one in that position the following year. You will also find it helpful to keep a record of your seeds: how many packets you used of each kind, how good the germination was, how many plants you grew, and how many you need. Although it can be wasteful on compost and propagator space to grow more than you need, you should err on the generous side when sowing your

Plant Supports

Plant supports are vital for some varieties (see Plant Directory), in order to prevent them from blowing over and the flowers from spoiling. A tidy row of well-supported plants will not only save you the irritation of having to try to tie them up in a gale, but will also make the job of picking them easier and quicker. If you have just a few plants in your beds or borders use twigs, herbaceous supports or bamboos and string.

STAKING

For large plants in rows, such as *Centaurea macrocephala*, achillea and eryngiums, use wooden stakes or strong bamboos and thick twine. (Discarded baler twine is very strong and durable.)

Do remember the potential danger to eyes when working among rows and clumps supported by bamboo sticks. The canes can be hidden in the foliage and you may not see them. Some people put old ping-pong balls on the tops of sticks; special protectors are available.

HERBACEOUS SUPPORTS

For individual clumps, use herbaceous supports. They can either be made out of galvanized wire, or they can be bought. Watch the plants as they grow, and make sure that in the early stages all the stems are tucked into the supports, as it is not easy to do this later when you will probably break the stems. When the clumps are well grown the supports are hidden, and are left in place until the dead foliage is cut down in the autumn.

NETTING

For some rows of plants such as *Helichrysum bracteatum* 'Monstrosum', ammobium, xeranthemum and cornflowers, plastic bean and pea nets cut into lengths and attached to bamboos provide excellent support. These nets have large mesh, usually 5in² (12.5cm²), of which two squares wide are suitable for the large helichrysums and three for the ammobium, xeranthemum, cornflowers and carthamus. You will see how many horizontal rows are necessary as the plants grow, usually one or two, sometimes three. Get the first layer on in good time. Fix it to the bamboos with a plastic tie so you can move it up as the

An acanthus, seen here in front of Eryngium tripartitum, *needs sturdy support.*

The bamboos and netting must be fixed before the plants grow to their full size.

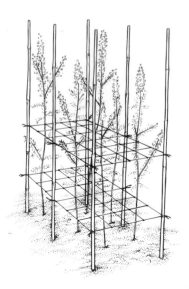

Layers of plastic nets provide good support for some taller plants.

plants grow, and add any subsequent layers as necessary. Do not have the final layer too high or it will interfere with your picking, and you may inadvertently cut the net.

When the plants are finished in the autumn do not try to pull the nets off; they will be entwined with the stems and you will only break the mesh. Rather, cut through the stems between each layer of net and pull out the dead foliage. The nets can then be rolled up and stored for future use. They will last for many years if treated carefully, and are very inexpensive.

Weed Control

This is a contentious subject! There are many tried and tested ways of dealing with these great survivors, which despite all the best efforts seem always to be around. However well made, your compost heap will inevitably contain some weed seeds, and, of course, the wind and birds spread them. Many lovers of flowers have a fondness for some weeds, considering them to be a 'plant in the wrong place'. As long as they are no nuisance they can be very charming and even of use. For example, wild field poppies have little seed pods which can look very attractive in some smaller arrangements.

Others, however, have to be dealt with ruthlessly. Chickweed, groundsel, shepherd's purse, fat hen, land cress and many more must be removed before they set seed, and are put on the compost heap. Hand weeding, or careful hoeing, is a chore that still has to be done if your seedlings are to flourish. It is as well to

remember that weed, and some plant seeds, can remain dormant for many years in the soil, and to neglect your weeding is only to increase your work in future years.

Inevitably, sometimes a clump of flowers becomes so choked with grass or weeds that your only option is to lift it in the autumn or spring. Divide it carefully, endeavouring to remove every piece of the offending weed. Conveniently, the roots of couch grass and bindweed are white and show up well, which helps, but you will have to watch for signs that some has been missed, and be ready to deal with it if any reappears at some later date.

Never pull up couch grass, bindweed or ground elder when weeding. You will only break the root and the remaining portion will soon sprout and your problems will start all over again. The same applies to dandelions and docks; it is much better to paint them with weed killer if you cannot guarantee removing all of the tap root.

WEEDKILLERS

Feelings about weedkillers are mixed, but if properly used glyphosate is perfectly safe and is rendered inactive the moment it touches the soil. You can save a lot of time and hard work by using it between rows of annuals and perennials, where you walk, when watering or picking. Use a watering can fitted with a watering bar. Keep the can solely for this purpose and clearly mark it 'Weedkiller' to prevent others from using it accidently with disastrous results. Follow the instructions on the packet meticulously, and with great care you can safely apply the weedkiller to within 2–3in (5–7.5cm) of the plants. The paths will stay clear of weeds and you will be saved unnecessary hoeing.

Glyphosate can also be used on weeds with large leaves, such as dock, dandelions and coltsfoot. Make up a solution in a jam jar which has a screw-top lid and, using a 1in (2.5cm) paintbrush, carefully paint the liquid onto the leaves, making sure none runs off onto any plants near by. Add some wallpaper paste to thicken the mixture, or buy prepared glyphosate in its own container, which has a brush in the lid. Wear thick rubber gloves when doing this job, and screw the lid onto the jar when walking between areas that need attention, thus preventing spilling the contents accidentally. 'Painting' weeds like this is particularly effective if done on a sunny day. There is no point in applying weedkiller when you know rain is imminent, or if the leaves are wet.

Touch-weed sticks are also effective if used on plants such as dock and dandelion which have large, thick leaves. For couch grass you can use alloxydim sodium which is helpful in controlling and weakening the growth of this invasive weed, but it does not entirely remove it.

WEED GLOVES
These are splendid for eradicating weeds in clumps of herbaceous plants. Wearing the heaviest rubber glove you can buy, and then putting over this a thick woollen or cotton glove, dip your hand into a mixture of glyphosate and squeeze hard to remove any excess liquid. Then stroke any couch grass or weeds that cannot be removed from a clump of herbaceous plants, or are difficult to reach. The effect is magical; very soon the offending weed will wither and die,

In a full bed or border, a weed glove may be the only way to get rid of unwelcome weeds.

having absorbed the herbicide which then works down to the roots and kills it. Be careful that the stroked weeds do not hang down and touch any flowers or foliage. The time and frustration this method saves is remarkable, and has proved to be most effective, particularly for the frustratingly persistent couch grass and ground elder.

MULCHES
A most effective way to cut down the endless chore of weeding beds and borders is to cover all the bare soil with a 2in (5cm) mulch of tree bark. There are several brands available, each offering a range of fine to coarse. Such weeds that come through are very easy to pull out, saving hours of work. It is expensive, but if you buy more than just a few bags you will probably get a discount, and it will prove money well spent. The mulch, as already mentioned, also helps to conserve moisture in dry summers.

CUTTING
AND DRYING

It is always an exciting moment when your first flowers are ready (these will probably be the polygonum and Alchemilla mollis) but it has to be said that if you are growing on a large scale, by the end of the season you will never want to see a dried flower again!

Basic Equipment

SECATEURS
Do choose these carefully. Remember that you are picking and not pruning with them. They must be strong, as they will be in continuous use, and although the daily work load on them will almost certainly prove to be too much after a few years, they must be light. Your wrist will be under as much strain as the secateurs, and a heavy pair will only leave it stiff and aching after a long

ABOVE: *Harvesting a good crop of* Delphinium consolida *(larkspur).*
PREVIOUS PAGES 28–29: *A carpet of dried flowers.*

Equipment for wiring roses and helichrysums, and for bunching smaller flowers such as cornflowers:
1 *Thick stub wire;* **2** *Thin stub wire;* **3** *Butchers' hooks;* **4** *Rubber bands;* **5** *Rolls of florists' wire;* **6** *Wire cutters.*

cutting session. They must fit your hand comfortably with a good grip. Try the secateurs out in the shop by opening and closing them to see that they are well balanced and feel right. Flower cutters that hold the stem so that you can pick one-handed are useful, although in crowded rows the blades can get caught up in the flower stems.

You will also need a good strong pair for cutting thick-stemmed plants, such as echinops and teasels, and for pruning your herbaceous plants. Your usual garden secateurs will be quite adequate for this, but will need sharpening before you prune your roses. There is an implement available for doing this, or you can have them professionally sharpened. A holster for your light secateurs is a great help, so that you do not need to keep putting them down every time you secure a bunch of flowers.

BASKETS
Baskets for putting the cut flowers in are invaluable. A light one can be used for smaller flowers, and a wicker log basket which is very strong can be used for carrying bulky material such as teasels and artichokes. Baskets need to be flat so that you can lay the bunches down. Do not put too many bunches on top of each other, or you will crush the lower ones. Round baskets can be awkward, as the bunches tend to fall over, and the heads can droop and be badly damaged.

RUBBER BANDS
You need these for securing the bunches, and you will require three sizes, small, medium, and large, strong ones. The small size is useful for plants such as cornflowers, ammobium and rhodanthe; the medium for alchemilla and acroclinium; and the large ones for

Flat-bottomed baskets are the best type for harvesting flowers.

teasels and echinops. Plastic containers are best used for storing the rubber bands as they do not rust when placed on damp grass, and the lids will prevent spillage when you are moving around the garden. Keep some bands on your fingers, in a pocket, or on your wrist, to avoid having to make endless trips up the rows to fetch more when you are busy bunching the flowers.

Harvesting the Flowers

If you pick in good time, your flowers will keep their colour well. Advice on timing is giving for each variety in the Plant Directory. So many dried flowers on sale are dyed because they have been picked too late and have lost their natural colour. If you pick on time, this won't be necessary – and natural colours are so much more attractive.

Always pick on a sunny or windy day, so that the flowers are dry. It is rarely possible to pick before lunch as the dew can be heavy and takes time to evaporate. Flowers picked when moist and then bunched will only go mouldy, and you are wasting your time and material by doing so. If the summer is persistently wet, though, and you are forced to pick the flowers when they are damp, bunch them loosely in small numbers, and then hang them over your boiler or in your airing cupboard. Watch them carefully, and remove them to a warm and airy

The result of an afternoon's harvesting – bunches of gypsophila, Limonium sinuatum (statice), Ammobium alatum grandiflorum and eryngiums ready to be dried.

room as soon as you know all the moisture has evaporated, and before they open too far.

BUNCHING
Strip off all the leaves, unless indicated otherwise in the Plant Directory. It is much easier to remove them at this stage. If left until later, the leaves go limp and are difficult to strip off the stems.

Do not bunch together too many flowers or the ones on the inside will be crushed, and by not getting enough air circulating around them they may go mouldy. An indication of the ideal number of stems to bunch together is provided in the Plant Directory. Ensure the ends are even – cut them if necessary – and slip on a rubber band, twisting it around the end of the bunch until it is just tight enough to hold them securely. The soft stems shrink as they dry, so the bands need to be tight enough to stop the flowers falling out later.

Helichrysums

You should cut all your flowers' stems – with the exception of helichrysums. The only way to pick these easily and quickly is by using your fingers. Pinch off the heads leaving ½–¾in (12–18mm) of stem, and put these in a small basket or trug. It will save time later if you keep the colours separately, especially if you are gathering a large quantity. The stems stain your fingers and thumb nail, so use a good barrier cream, working it under your fingernails. It is then easily washed off, and any persistent stain can be removed using an orange stick tipped with cotton wool and dipped in cuticle remover.

You can, of course, cut the heads off if you prefer, but it is a very slow process. The 'Bikini' varieties of helichrysums do not have long enough stems to be able to leave these on. 'Monstrosum' do have

Nipping off the head of a helichrysum.

Freshly gathered Delphinium consolida *(larkspur).*

long stems, but they go limp very quickly and hang their heads if there is any damp. They may be adequate for your own floral arrangements, but not if you want to sell them.

WIRING

After picking, helichrysums can be left for a few hours, but then they will have to be wired. For this you need two gauges of stub wire: a fine 22-gauge cut into 7in (17.5cm) lengths for the 'Bikini' heads, and a longer, thicker 20-gauge cut into 10in (25cm) lengths for the 'Monstrosum' variety.

Remove any remaining leaves and then nip each stem cleanly ¼–½in (6–12mm) below the head. Then carefully push the wire into the stem and just into the base of the head. Do not allow the wire to come out through the top of the head, or it will show. This procedure is not nearly as tricky as it sounds, and you will soon become proficient. Wiring may sound a tedious business, but you will soon become adept, and it is a great help if you have help. Two of you, one to nip off the heads, and the other to wire, will halve the time taken.

DRYING

Put the wired stems into bunches of ten, bending the wires a little so that the heads do not touch, and slip on a small rubber band, twisting it round a few times until the bunch is held firmly. Use two bands for the longer wires, one near the top and one near the bottom of the bunch, so that the wires do not splay out and get tangled. Bend down the end of one wire, and hang the bunch up to dry in a warm, airy room, or in the airing cupboard for a day if you think the heads may be at all damp.

Wiring helichrysum heads.

Helipterum hung up to dry.

When you are sure the flowers are quite dry, store them in a well-ventilated room, away from bright sunlight. The wires will stick firmly to the stems as the flowers dry, but care is needed for the first few days when moving the bunches in case the heads fall off before this has happened.

CAUTIONARY NOTE
Some books will tell you that you can wire helichrysum heads when they are dry. Do not be fooled: it cannot be done successfully or safely. Once the heads are dry, they become very hard and any remaining stem will have shrivelled. You will have to try and force the wire right through each helichrysum head, hooking it over the top so that it does not slip out again. This will almost certainly result in crushed heads, in which the wire will show, and, more seriously, you will run the very real risk of pushing the wire not just into the flower head, but into your finger. This is not only painful, but also dangerous, for the result will be a 'puncture' wound, with all the risk of subcutaneous infection.

Drying and Preserving

HANG DRYING
Always remember that damp is death to dried flowers. Average drying times are indicated in the Plant Directory, but much will depend on the summer, the amount of warmth in your drying room, and the moisture in the flowers when they are picked. Experience should tell you when they are fully dry, but the

general rule is that they are ready when they feel papery, and the heads do not bend over when held upright.

Old laundry rails on pulleys that can be raised and lowered in a warm kitchen or workroom are ideal for hanging up bunches. You can also use free-standing clothes airers, or curtain rails in a bright, but not too sunny window (if you do not mind being unable to close the curtains at night). Hooks on walls can be used, too, although they are not ideal because the air cannot circulate freely around the bunch and the flowers resting against the wall may get crushed. However, they are satisfactory for plants such as teasels. For smaller flowers, such as rhodanthe, ammobium and others, put two bunches together with a rubber band, hang them over a wire coat hanger, and suspend it from a rail while they dry.

Do not overcrowd the bunches as they need plenty of air to circulate round them, and do not hang them in a very sunny window or the colours will fade and the flowers will open too far. On fine days, leave a window open to allow plenty of air to circulate, and to reduce the risk of infection by mould.

Some flowers need to be dried quickly after they are picked, and these, too, are indicated in the Plant Directory. Hang these over your boiler or in the airing cupboard for the recommended period. *Never* be tempted to put your bunches straight into a shed or garage, however hot the summer, as moisture at night and in the early morning will affect them.

STORAGE

You will need a good dry room where you can place your bunches once they are really dry. Heat is not necessary, or desirable, at this stage, but the store must not be damp. Until the late summer, it can be worth letting air in on sunny or windy days, but after that keep all windows and doors firmly shut. Trays of silica gel and moisture-attracting containers can be helpful in reducing humidity in a storeroom. You can also buy electric de-humidifiers, but these are expensive and should only be necessary if you are growing on a very large scale. A small fan heater set to cold, and turned on for an hour or so occasionally, is excellent, as it keeps the air circulating. Do not set it to hot, as the heat will make the flowers open too much, and some will become over-dried and brittle. It is safe to hang teasels in a garage or shed once dry, but they are the only variety that can be stored in this way.

Flowers can also be stored in cupboards, attics (if dry) and in boxes under beds if these are not over-filled. A word of warning to those of you who keep cats: they find the flowers irresistible, so make sure they cannot get at them.

BORAX AND SILICA GEL

Drying flowers using these methods is time-consuming and requires skill and patience. The results can be excellent, but the flowers are extremely fragile and are suitable only for your own use. Many varieties of flowers can be preserved in this way; the most successful are roses with small, tight blooms – pick them either when in bud or with half- to fully open heads.

Pick the heads when they are quite dry. Place an inch of borax (available from a chemist) in the bottom of a box – a shoe box is ideal. Hold the flower over the box and, using a fine sieve, gently shake more borax in between all the petals until the head is quite covered.

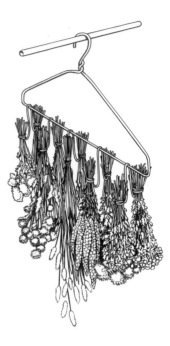

Smaller flowers can be bunched and hung from a wire coat hanger and left to dry.

Large plants such as artichokes, leek heads and teasels can be hung on wall hooks.

Lay the flower in the box. Repeat the process with more flowers, being careful not to overcrowd them, and leaving plenty of room between the blooms. Finally, cover the flowers completely with more borax, put the lid on the box and place it somewhere warm, such as in the airing cupboard.

After 5–8 days, open the box; very gently lift out each flower. Care is needed as they are not easy to find in the borax. Gently shake each flower, using a fine paintbrush to remove any borax from between the petals.

Store the flowers in another box, and keep them somewhere warm, but not too hot. Stems of roses will probably be strong enough for arranging, but other flowers may need their heads wiring, which is best done before drying (see page 31). Keep borax in a dry, warm place when not in use.

Silica gel crystals can be used in the same way as borax, but they need to be ground to a fine powder (do not inhale this) using a food mixer, or crushing with a rolling pin.

You can speed up the drying time when using silica gel by using a microwave oven. At 300 watts (No. 4) setting, drying material using, for example, ½lb (225g) of crystals will take 2–2½ minutes, whereas 2¼lb (1.2kg) will take 5–6 minutes.

Because the crystals absorb moisture, they should be regularly dried out in an ordinary oven. Their colour changes from blue to pink indicating when this is necessary. Do not dry too much at one time. At setting 375°F/190°C/gas 5, 1–2lb (450g–1kg) will take about 30 minutes. Borax, however, if kept in an airing cupboard, never needs drying out and is far less trouble.

GLYCERINE

Many leaves can be preserved using glycerine. Beech, sweet chestnut, mahonia, eucalyptus and box can all be used, but other leaves tend to produce varying results. Sometimes oak and laurel take the solution well. Remember that it is mainly the thicker leaves that do best.

To make the solution, mix one part glycerine to two parts hot, but not boiling, water. Pour the glycerine into a large jar. Gently pour the water onto the glycerine, mixing it well. Have the stems ready and place them in the mixture, having split the stems vertically 1–2in (2.5–5cm) at the base; remove any leaves that may be submerged in the solution as they will go mouldy. Make sure you have enough mixture as it is surprising how much is absorbed, and be sure that all the stems are well down in the glycerine. You may have to top up the solution after a few days. Do not leave the material in the mixture too long, or the leaves will start to exude glycerine and become sticky. Eucalyptus and box will not change colour significantly, but others will turn a dark shade of brown.

LENGTH OF TIME IN SOLUTION
Beech: 7–10 days
Sweet chestnut: 8–15 days
Eucalyptus; Box;
Oak; Mahonia; Laurel: 2–4 weeks

When the leaves are ready, remove them from the solution, dry the ends, and store them flat between newspaper, or in large boxes. They will keep for several years and can be used over and over again in arrangements.

The arrangement on the windowsill includes hydrangeas, beech leaves, Stachys lanata, Delphinium consolida (larkspur), helichrysums, hops,

Limonium suworowii (pink pokers), Amaranthus caudatus *(Love-lies-bleeding) and* Eryngium giganteum; *the basket on the table contains* Moluccella laevis, Carlina acaulis, Alchemilla mollis, Delphinium consolida *(larkspur),* Helipterum manglesii, roses, poppy heads, Stachys lanata *and* Amaranthus hypochondriacus 'Green Thumb'. *The basket on the wall features* Nigella orientalis, *eucalyptus, helichrysums,* Limonium sinuatum *(statice), roses and gypsophila.*

ARRANGING
DRIED FLOWERS

Once you have successfully planted, nurtured, harvested and dried your chosen plants, you can group them into attractive arrangements for year-round enjoyment. First, you will need to gather together suitable containers and the necessary equipment.

Basic Equipment

CONTAINERS
The choice of suitable containers for dried flowers is extensive, but bear in mind that glass vases show the foam and stems. Baskets always look attractive, and copper, brass, earthenware and wooden boxes lend themselves well to dried flower arrangements.

FOAM, FOAM HOLDERS AND GUM
The standard green foam, used dry for dried flowers, is excellent. (Do not use the brown foam if you are using flowers with brittle stems.) Hold the foam in place with a plastic spike itself held in

A selection of pottery jars suitable for dried flower arrangements.

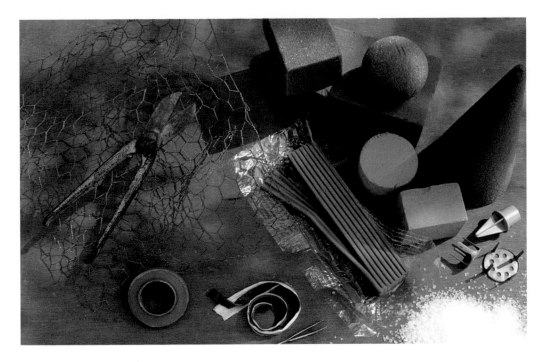

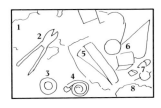

Equipment for arranging dried flowers: **1** *Chicken wire;* **2** *Wire cutters;* **3** *Florists' tape;* **4** *Foam fix;* **5** *Plasticine;* **6** *Arrangers' foam;* **7** *Foam supports;* **8** *Silica gel.*

place with a piece of florist's gum. When using baskets, wire the foam in position through the wicker.

WIRE NETTING AND TAPE

For large arrangements, which require extra support, place a piece of galvanized or plastic-covered wire netting over the top. The wire should have mesh measuring $1–2in^2$ ($2.5–5cm^2$) for positioning large stems into the foam. Hold it in place with adhesive florist's tape, which comes in various colours, using one piece from back to front, and one from side to side, sticking the ends under the rim of the container. The ends can be hidden with a piece of foliage or a flower when making the arrangement.

WIRE CUTTERS

A small pair is necessary for cutting florist's wire. Buy them from florists' suppliers or from a hardware store.

TWEEZERS

When making small arrangements using individual, delicate flowers, a pair of tweezers is invaluable. Fly-tying tweezers, measuring 5in (12.5cm) long, are excellent. Hold the stem firmly in the tweezers and then push it into the foam. In this way you can reach parts of the arrangement that you may not otherwise be able to get at with your fingers.

WEIGHTS

Remember that there will be no water to lend weight to your arrangement so keeping it stable. Pebbles and stones of various sizes can be used as weights around the foam in the base of the container. Sand, too, can be used, but wherever you obtain it from, be sure to wash it well, and make sure it is dry before placing it in your container. The time spent in securing your basic foundations is essential.

PREVIOUS PAGES 40–41: *The wreath includes oats, wheat, oak leaves, hops and* Physalis franchetii *(Chinese lanterns); the swag contains hops, oat, wheat,* Physalis franchetii *(Chinese lanterns),* Helipterum humboldtianum *and* Delphinium consolida *(larkspur). In the jug are* Moluccella laevis, Nigella damascena, Achillea filipendulina, Carthamus tinctorius, *hydrangeas and* Craspedia globosa.

This arrangement features helichrysums, Delphinium consolida *(larkspur), oats,* Ammobium alatum grandiflorum, Centaurea cyanus *(cornflowers),* Carthamus tinctorius, Nigella damascena, Anaphalis *and* Achillea filipendulina.

b. If the stem is not strong enough to do this, first carefully push a fine stub wire measuring 4–6in (10–15cm) long into the stem, and then insert the end of the wire into a larger stem. The wire alone may be enough for the length you need, but if the head is heavy, like those of carlinas or artichokes, you will need a very strong extender to bear the weight.

Stem wrap comes in several shades of green and brown, and is self-adhesive. Cover any visible wire with stem wrap, and also use it to make sure the join of wire and extender is secure. It is particularly useful for wired helichrysums if the wires are likely to be visible in the finished arrangement.

SPRAYS

Poppy seed heads, artichokes, fir cones, teasels and other material such as nuts, can all be sprayed gold or silver for Christmas decorations using aerosol cans of paint. Various shades of copper, gold and silver are available.

Before spraying, fir cones and nuts will have to be wired. For cones, wind a wire around the base of the cone. Nuts are rather tricky, however, but if you can make a small hole in the base you can insert a wire, having put a blob of glue on the end of the wire first.

Stick the stems of the material you want to spray into a large, old piece of foam, which has been fixed securely into an old tin. Spread newspapers under the tin, and around the back and sides (if you do not want to spray your walls!). Try to do this work in a garage or workroom with good ventilation, as the paint gives off very strong fumes. If you have to do it in the house, make sure you open a window, and leave it open until no trace of the smell remains.

EXTENDERS AND STEM WRAP

Do not throw away all the cut-off portions of dried stems. When you are forming your arrangement, you may need to lengthen some of the flowers, and this can be done in two ways:

a. If the stem to be extended is small and strong, such as those of pink pokers or xeranthemum, cut the end at an angle and push it into a larger stem with a hollow or pithy centre.

An arrangement including hydrangeas, beech leaves, Amaranthus caudatus *(Love-lies-bleeding) and helichrysums.*

Shake the can of paint very vigorously, and then spray the material lightly, giving it a second coat after a few minutes if necessary. Turn the stem container round several times so that you reach all sides of the material.

Experiment with various types of seed heads. Old grasses that have lost their colour, wheat in particular, take spray very well, as do carlinas and carthamus.

A squirt of hair spray helps prevent bulrushes from bursting open when dry, and echinops and scabiosa 'Drumstick' from shattering (see pages 122, 123).

CLEANING UP

A large, old tablecloth or piece of strong plastic sheeting put on the floor is vital to protect your carpets if you are arranging *in situ*. This makes the job of sweeping up afterwards much easier. Small pieces of dried flowers stick to carpets and upholstery with a tenacity that defeats the most powerful cleaner. Keep a large plastic bin-liner beside you when doing large arrangements in churches and elsewhere, as this makes the final clearing up less of a chore. If you are delivering dried flowers in your car it is advisable to cover the seats with a cloth or sheeting, as it is extremely difficult to remove any bits from the upholstery.

Flower Arrangements

This is primarily a book on how to grow dried flowers, so it does not go into great detail on all the aspects of arranging. However, a few basic principles may be helpful for those of you who would like to create your own arrangements.

MAKING THE OUTLINE

Try to imitate nature. Look at plants and flowers and observe how they grow; buds and tapered ends of leaves are usually at the top of a plant, and the heavier leaves and open flower heads are further down, or at the base. Use grasses, pink pokers and bistort, for example, to mark out the general outline of your arrangement. A good basic principle to follow is:

One and a half times the height of the container plus the width.

The Japanese practitioners of Ikebana use a system of Heaven, Man and Earth (see right) to achieve a pleasing balance, and this is a formula that works well in any arrangement.

FILLING OUT

Having made your outline, you can begin to add the rest of the flowers. First put in place any flowers that have brittle stems which are likely to break, such as *Helipterum roseum* (acroclinium). Add the prickly varieties next: eryngium, carlinas and teasels can catch on delicate flowers if added later, causing them to break. If using helichrysums, leave them to the last as they can be inserted easily anywhere in the arrangement.

Small flowers such as *Helichrysum cassinianum* and *H. subulifolium*, cornflowers, and ammobium are easier to cope with if they are first made into small bunches using three, five or seven flowers secured with fine florist's wire. Heavier-headed flowers should be placed at the base. Not only does this look more natural, but if placed high up, they can make an arrangement unstable. Finally, fill in the spaces using statice, grasses, glycerined leaves, and any other material that is suitable.

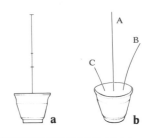

a *The height of your arrangement should be one and a half times the height of the container plus the width.*

b A *Heaven* B *Man* C *Earth*

c *To ensure a stable arrangement, place the heavier leaves and flower heads towards the base.*

d *Small flowers are easier to cope with if they are first wired into bunches of up to seven flowers.*

A bedside table arrangement featuring delphiniums, artichokes, Craspedia globosa, Centaurea macrocephala, Solidago candensis, Carthamus tinctorius, *helichrysums,* Gypsophila paniculata *'Bristol Fairy',* Carlina acaulis, Achillea filipendulina *and* Eryngium alpinum.

If you can, always create your arrangement *in situ*. Moving a large, heavy container through doors and along passages to its final resting place is fraught with difficulties and even danger.

FLORAL WICKER BASKETS
Bunches of dried flowers look particularly attractive when grouped together. Closely pack together a selection of bunches in a wicker basket to achieve a stunning effect. No foam or framework is needed to hold them in place. Small flowers such as ammobium, cornflowers, dumosa, *Helichrysum subulifolium* and lavender look especially good in these baskets.

DECORATIVE BALLS
These balls are particularly attractive for Christmas, using red helichrysums and small pieces of red ribbon twisted round a piece of wire. To make, tie a piece of ribbon around a foam ball and knot it at the top, leaving enough ribbon to make a large loop from which to hang the ball.

Use firm-stemmed material cut short – 1–2in (2.5–5cm) of stem is ample – and cover the ball with small helichrysums, little pieces of achillea, wired fir cones, seed heads, xeranthemums, ammobium and other material. Finish with pieces of dumosa or gypsophila. Tweezers are helpful when pushing the softer stems into the foam.

LAVENDER BASKETS

These smell delicious and look most attractive. Other herbs to use are pot marjoram, tansy, thyme, and the heads of dried mint flowers. Tightly fill baskets as above, or, if you prefer, fix a block of foam in the basket and arrange the herbs individually.

To make lavender 'scent bottles', simply fold down the heads of lavender and then thread ribbon through the stems, as shown opposite.

POMANDERS

Sweet-smelling pomanders are always a delight. They can be made simply by placing herbs into a foam ball as described for the decorated balls on page 47.

MINIATURE TREES

A different way to arrange dried flowers is in the shape of a small orange tree. Take a new, or very clean, terracotta pot and fill it with wet plaster (or a large portion of florist's plasticine). Into this, insert a length of wooden dowelling, around which you have wrapped ribbon. Wait until the plaster is quite dry and set, and then gently push a foam ball onto the top of the dowelling. Cover it with a selection of small flower heads, fir cones, seed pods and glycerined box leaves and dumosa.

This arrangement features Limonium sinuatum, Helipterum manglesii, *gypsophila*, Limonium tataricum *'Dumosa'*, *xeranthemum*, Catananche caerulea *and lavender. Alongside are some lavender 'scent bottles' – these are easy to make and are very fragrant.*

FESTIVE WREATHS

Wreaths covered with dried flowers, fir cones, glycerined leaves and other material are charming. Red ribbon bows and small coloured balls can be added at Christmas time. Foam-filled wreath bases of different sizes can easily be bought. Tie a piece of ribbon around the top, leaving enough length to make a large loop. Cover the foam with a selection of material of your choice.

SWAGS

Rope is an excellent basis from which to work, as it hangs gracefully. Working from one end, tie on small bunches of flowers ensuring that the stems of the first bunch are covered by the heads of the second, and so on. Continue until you have covered the whole length of the rope. Tie string or ribbon round the ends of the rope so that you can hang it up. Helichrysums, fir cones and other wired materials can be pushed through the rope, or wound around it. Ribbon, balls and tinsel can all be incorporated into the swag at Christmas time.

POSIES

At weddings, small dried flower posies and table arrangements can be given to guests as permanent mementos of the occasion. A bride who wishes to keep her bouquet often likes to have one made of small dried flowers and tiny dried rosebuds.

Posy holders with foam set in the top can be filled with dried flowers; or bind the stems of a small bunch of flowers with stem wrap and cover this with ribbon to make an attractive finish for carrying the posy. Dumosa and gypsophila add charm to small bouquets, as do rosebuds made out of ribbon.

FIREPLACES

During the summer months, fireplaces make ideal locations for large arrangements of dried flowers. The only room where they are not suitable is the bathroom, as the damp atmosphere there will cause the flowers to droop and, eventually, to go mouldy.

The flowers in the jug include pompom dahlias, Lunaria annua (honesty), Matricaria grandiflora, Delphinium consolida (larkspur) and Eryngium tripartitum.

TABLE CENTRES

Silver containers are ideal for table centres, but be careful when using them, for they are easy to scratch. Place a small plastic tub containing foam fixed with a foam holder inside the container. The whole arrangement can then be lifted out in order to clean the container.

A table centre arrangement should be round or oval in shape, as it will be seen from all angles, and it should not be too tall. Fill it with flowers of your choice. Borax-dried roses, dumosa and other small flowers are ideal, with a few small glycerined mahonia leaves to outline the arrangement.

The table centre includes helichrysums, Icelandic moss, hops and Ammobium alatum grandiflorum. *Hanging up are helichrysums, gypsophila,* Linum usitatissimum *and setaria.*

PLANT DIRECTORY

Before you stock your garden you will want
to have as much information as you can get
on all the varieties of plants suitable for
drying. Thus armed, you can proceed with
confidence to cultivate good-quality,
beautiful flowers which will be an
everlasting reminder of happy times spent
in your garden.

The botanical illustrations throughout the Plant
Directory show each plant *after* it has been dried.

ANNUALS

1 *Amaranthus caudatus;*
2 *Amaranthus viridis.*

RIGHT: *Amaranthus*
hypochondriacus
'Green Thumb'

KEY FOR ANNUALS

(HH) = Half-hardy:
withstands temperatures
down to 32°F (0°C)
(H) = Hardy:
withstands temperatures
down to 23°F (−5°C)

Amaranthus
LOVE-LIES-BLEEDING

A. caudatus (HH) S America
Height: 1–2½ft (30–75cm)
Colour: Red

A. hypochondriacus (HH)
S America
Variety: 'Pygmy Torch'
Height: 1ft (30cm)
Colour: Crimson
Variety: 'Green Thumb'
Height: 2ft (60cm)
Colour: Green

A. viridis (HH) S America
Height: 1–2½ft (30–75cm)
Colour: Green

How to grow: Can be sown outside in mild areas in early spring, or in seed trays in a greenhouse or on a windowsill. Maintain a temperature of 59°F (15°C). The germination rate is very good, so half seed trays are adequate. Prick out into seed trays or polystyrene sectioned trays, harden off in a cold frame and plant out in late spring or early summer, leaving 1ft (30cm) between plants and 1½ft

(45cm) between rows. These plants prefer good soil, in a well-drained, sunny position. Feed weekly with soluble fertilizer high in potash.

Staking: Not necessary.
Pests and diseases: Usually trouble free.

When to cut: When the tassels are well formed and of good colour. With the larger varieties, you can pick the main head and the side branches separately; the smaller varieties are best picked as one spray.
Drying: Pick off the leaves and either hang individually for the larger varieties, or in bunches of 3–5 stems for the smaller. Some heat is helpful.
Drying time: 5–10 days.
Arranging: When dry, the heads of varieties 'Pygmy Torch' and 'Green Thumb' stay upright, but the other varieties will droop.

Ammobium

A. alatum grandiflorum
(HH) Australia
Height: 2–4ft (60–120cm)
Colour: White with yellow centres

How to grow: In a greenhouse or on a windowsill. Germination is good, so half seed trays are adequate. Maintain a temperature of 65°F (18°C). Prick out into sectioned trays, harden off and plant out in late spring or early summer in double, staggered rows, leaving 1ft (30cm) between plants and 1ft (30cm) between each double row. Prefers good soil, in a well-drained and sunny position. Feed with liquid fertilizer high in potash for good blooms.

Staking: Yes. Nets and bamboos.
Pests and diseases: Can be attacked by aphids. Spray with an insecticide of your choice.
When to cut: As soon as the flowers are open, with yellow centres, or delay until the centres start to turn brown. Do not leave too long, as some centres will become too dark. Cut only short stems with flowers, usually about 8–10in (20–25cm) long, to encourage side shoots and buds. Plants continue to flower until the first frosts, and in some areas, in milder winters, survive to flower again the following year.
Drying: Bunch together 20–30 stems and hang upside down to dry. Heat is not necessary, but a warm room is advisable.
Drying time: 1–1½ weeks.
Arranging: Use individually in very small arrangements or bunch together 5–10 stems with fine florist's wire, and place in larger arrangements.

Carthamus SAFFLOWER

C. tinctorius (H) Mediterranean
Height: 2–5ft (60–150cm)
Colour: Green heads with yellow or
orange petals

How to grow: This is a most attractive
plant. The heads have a ruff of green
leaves round a tight bud, which opens
to reveal yellow or orange petals. Sow
in seed trays in a greenhouse or on a
windowsill. Maintain a temperature of
60–70°F (16–21°C). Prick out into
sectioned trays, harden off and plant
out when safe to do so, leaving 1ft
(30cm) between plants and 1½ft
(45cm) between rows. A weekly foliar
feed is beneficial.

Staking: If the plants grow tall, yes.
Bamboos and nets.
Pests and diseases: Can be attacked by
aphids. Spray with an insecticide of
your choice.

When to cut: Some years these plants
grow very tall, and only mature in late
summer, with the risk of early frosts
damaging the heads. However, many
people prefer to pick them before the
orange flowers appear, as soon as the
heads are fully formed and feel hard.
If they are ready in good time and you
want the orange petals, leave till these
are just appearing and pick then; or
pick a whole spray. In this way, you
will get a mixture of green and green-
and-orange heads.
Drying: Bunch together 3–5 sprays
and hang upside down to dry. Some
heat is advisable. The heads last well,
and can also be sprayed gold for
Christmas decorations.
Drying time: 1–3 weeks.
Arranging: A most useful flower, as
you can either use whole sprays in
large arrangements, or cut individual
stems for use in smaller arrangements.

Carthamus tinctorius

Centaurea CORNFLOWER

C. cyanus (H) British Isles
Height: 2–4ft (60–120cm)
Colour: Blue, pink, purple and white

How to grow: Sow outside in spring in a sunny position, in well-drained soil in double rows, 1ft (30cm) apart. Thin the seedlings out to 8–10in (20–25cm). Germination is good, so do not sow too thickly. Flowers prolifically, so short rows are adequate. Foliar feed for good blooms, and nip off some side shoots to get good-sized heads.

Staking: Yes. Nets and bamboos advised if a tall variety.

Pests and diseases: Usually trouble free.
When to cut: When the heads are from half- to fully open. Overripe flowers will drop their petals when dry. Pick each day.
Drying: Bunch together 10–12 stems and hang over the boiler or in an airing cupboard.
Drying time: 4–8 days, depending on how much heat is available. Only the blue flowers seem to dry well: the pink and purple ones are seldom successful and the white ones turn brown.
Arranging: Difficult to arrange individually; look more effective if 4–6 stems are bunched with fine florist's wire.

Centaurea cyanus

Craspedia

C. globosa (HH) Australasia
Height: 1–3ft (30–90cm)
Colour: Yellow

How to grow: This plant has strong stems bearing small round heads. Sow in seed trays in a greenhouse or on a windowsill. Germination results are variable. Maintain a temperature of 65–70°F (18–21°C). Prick out the seedlings into seed trays or sectioned trays, harden off, and plant out in early summer 8–12in (20–30cm) apart and leaving 1ft (30cm) between rows. Good soil, well drained and in a sunny position is preferred. For good-sized heads, feed if necessary with liquid fertilizer high in potash.

Staking: Some plants grow very tall, but staking is not usually needed.
Pests and diseases: Usually trouble free.
When to cut: When the heads are fully formed and of good colour.
Drying: Bunch together 10–15 stems and hang to dry. Heat is not necessary.
Drying time: 5–10 days.
Arranging: Useful in all arrangements.

Delphinium LARKSPUR

D. consolida (H) Europe
Height: 1½–4ft (45–120cm)
Colour: All shades

How to grow: Best sown in a greenhouse and pricked out into sectioned trays; but can be sown outside in early spring. In milder areas, sow in the autumn, protect in winter if necessary

by cloches; well-drained soil and a sunny position preferred. Sow in rows 1½–2ft (45–60cm) apart and thin seedlings to 9–12in (22.5–30cm) apart. Remove some side shoots to encourage good-sized blooms. Foliar feed weekly.

Staking: May be necessary for taller varieties.
Pests and diseases: Usually trouble free.

When to cut: When all but the top two or three florets are open.
Drying: Strip off leaves, bunch together 5–10 stems according to their size, and hang over a boiler or in an airing cupboard. Dry as quickly as possible.
Drying time: 5–10 days. Heat is advisable.
Arranging: A useful filler, and good for outlining arrangements.

Assorted delphiniums

Gomphrena
GLOBE AMARANTH

G. globosa (HH) India
Height: 1–2ft (30–60 cm)
Colour: Usually white and red/purple,
but yellow and orange strains available

How to grow: This plant does well in
warm areas, but in colder ones will
probably need to be kept in the
greenhouse in 5in (12.5cm) pots. The
round heads resemble clover. Sow in
seed trays in a greenhouse. Maintain a
temperature of 59–64°F (15–18°C).
Germination is variable. Prick out into
sectioned trays, harden off, and plant
out in spring when all danger of frost
has passed, 10in (25cm) apart, in rows
1ft (30cm) apart. A sunny position and
well-drained soil is preferable. Foliar
feed weekly, if necessary.

Staking: Not necessary.
Pests and diseases: Usually trouble
free.
When to cut: Just before the heads are
fully open, or when fully open.
Drying: Strip off leaves, bunch
together 12–18 stems and hang to dry.
Heat is not necessary.
Drying time: 5–10 days.
Arranging: Useful in small
arrangements.

Helichrysum
STRAWFLOWER

H. bracteatum (HH) Australia
Cultivar 'Bikini'
Height: 1–1½ft (30–45cm)
Colour: All shades
Cultivar 'Monstrosum'
Height: 3–5ft (90–150cm)
Colour: All shades

How to grow: This flower is probably
the best known of all dried flowers,
and some of the recently introduced
shades are lovely; they include pale
lemon yellow and a soft coral, neither
of which were previously obtainable.
Sow in half seed trays, as germination
is usually good, in a greenhouse or on
a windowsill. Maintain a temperature
of 64°F (18°C). Prick out into sectioned
trays or seed trays, harden off and
plant out when all danger of frost has
passed, in late spring or early summer.
Good, well-drained soil is preferred,
but this plant will tolerate most soils. A
sunny position is favoured. Foliar feed
weekly with fertilizer high in potash for
good blooms.

The 'Monstrosum' range grows to
great heights, so plant 1½–2ft
(45–60cm) apart and leave 2ft (60cm)
between rows. The 'Bikini' range
consists of short, compact plants, which
bear a prodigious number of blooms if
picked regularly. A few in a mixed bed
or border will give ample flowers for
your own use. If planting in rows, leave
1ft (30cm) between plants and rows.

Staking: 'Monstrosum': Yes. If in rows,
use bamboos and nets; if individual
plants, use herbaceous supports.
'Bikini': Not required.

Pests and diseases: Can be attacked by aphids in early summer. Watch carefully for this, and spray with a systemic insecticide of your choice.

When to cut: Most of the helichrysum on sale are a depressing sight, having been picked too late, and are therefore overblown. Pick as soon as the flowers begin to open but before they are fully extended. The heads will continue to open a little as they dry.

Drying: Nip off the heads leaving a stem of only ¼–½in (6–12mm) and wire as soon as possible (see page 34). When wired, bunch together not more than 10 and hang in a warm room to dry. If they are not absolutely dry when you have picked and wired them, hang them over the boiler or in an airing cupboard for a few hours, or even for a day. Do not hang them longer than this, however, or the heads will open too much.

Drying time: 5–10 days.

Arranging: Invaluable in all arrangements.

1 *Helichrysum bracteatum* 'Monstrosum';
2 *Helichrysum bracteatum* 'Bikini'.

Colourful helichrysums

Helichrysum

H. cassinianum (Pink cluster
everlasting) (HH) Australia
Height: 8–12in (20–30cm)
Colour: Pink

How to grow: A charming, fairly recent
introduction. A bushy little plant with
sprays of tiny pink flowers. Sow in
seed trays in a greenhouse or on a
windowsill. Maintain a temperature of
65°F (18°C). Germination is good, so
half trays may be sufficient. Prick out
into sectioned trays, harden off and
plant out when safe to do so in rows
1½ft (45cm) apart, leaving 1ft (30cm)
between plants. Well-drained soil in a
sunny position is preferred; feed
weekly with soluble fertilizer high in
potash for good blooms.

Staking: Not necessary.
Pests and Diseases: Seems to be
trouble free.
When to cut: This is a difficult plant to
pick. Some of the flowers will open at
the top of the little sprays, but if you
wait for the whole head to do so the
top ones will be overblown. Wait until
about half are open but some buds
remain, and then pick. It tends to be a
matter of trial and error, and personal
preference.
Drying: Strip off a few of the lower
leaves, bunch together 10–15 stems
and hang upside down to dry. Heat is
not necessary.
Drying Time: 7–10 days.
Arranging: They can be difficult to
arrange individually, and look better
wired into small bunches. They make
charming fillers.

Helichrysum

H. subulifolium cultivar 'Golden Star'
(HH) Australia
Height: 10–16in (25–40cm)
Colour: Yellow

How to grow: This plant has small, daisy-like flowers. Sow in a greenhouse or on a windowsill in seed trays. Germination is variable. Maintain a temperature of 65–70°F (18–21°C). Prick out into sectioned trays, harden off and plant out when safe to do so in rows 1ft (30cm) apart, leaving 8–10in (20–25cm) between plants. Well-drained soil and a sunny position is preferred. Feed weekly with soluble fertilizer high in potash for good blooms.

Staking: Not usually necessary, but some plants do tend to get a little top-heavy, in which case a small twig will usually be sufficient to support them.

Pests and diseases: Usually trouble free.

When to cut: When fully open. The first flowers will be the largest and strongest; the flowers will decrease in size as the plant matures. The later, smaller flowers are still useful.

Drying: Strip off any lower leaves; bunch together 10–20 stems and hang upside down to dry. Heat is not necessary, but a warm room is helpful.

Drying time: 6–10 days.

Arranging: Use individually in small arrangements, or bunch together 5–7 smaller flowers, using fine florist's wire.

Helichrysum subulifolium

Helipterum

H. roseum, syn. *Acroclinium roseum*
(H) Australia
Height: 1–1½ft (30–45cm)
Colour: White, pink and red

How to grow: A daisy-like flower with yellow or black centres. Sow outside in milder areas in spring, or in seed trays in a greenhouse or on a windowsill. Germination is usually good. Maintain a temperature of 61°F (16°C). Seeds can also be sown in polystyrene sectioned trays, two to three seeds to a section, later thinning out to strongest seedling. Pinch out the tip of the plant when 2–3in (5–7.5cm) high to avoid a lanky plant, and to encourage bushy growth. Harden off, and plant out in late spring leaving 1ft (30cm) between plants, and 1ft (30cm) between rows. Any well-drained soil and sunny position preferred; foliar feed weekly.

Staking: Not necessary.

Helipterum roseum

Pests and diseases: Can be attacked by aphids. Spray with an insecticide of your choice.
When to cut: As soon as the flowers are fully open.
Drying: Strip off the leaves, bunch together 15–20 stems and hang upside down to dry. Heat is not necessary but a warm room is advisable.
Drying time: 1–2 weeks.
Arranging: Useful in all arrangements, but care is needed, as some of the stems can be brittle.

Helipterum

H. humboldtianum (H) Australia
Height: 8–12in (20–30cm)
Colour: Yellow

How to grow: Clusters of tiny yellow flowers form the heads of this plant, which can be sown outside in milder areas in spring. In colder areas, grow as for *Helichrysum subulifolium*. This flower does not keep too well, but it is worth trying, and some years it does well.

Staking: Not necessary.
Pests and diseases: Usually trouble free.
When to cut: When the clusters start to open, but do not leave too long as the heads become rather untidy.
Drying: Bunch together 10–12 stems and hang upside down to dry.
Drying time: 7–10 days.
Arranging: Useful in small arrangements.

Helipterum

H. splendidum (HH) Australia
Height: 1–1½ft (30–45cm)
Colour: White

This plant is similar to *H. roseum* so
follow the instructions on page 66.
H. splendidum is a new introduction
and is a very attractive plant, having
strong stems and pretty flowers.
However, seeds can be difficult to
germinate.

Helipterum

H. manglesii, syn. *Rhodanthe manglesii* (H) Australia
Height: 1–1½ft (30–45cm)
Colour: White and pink

How to grow: This variety can also be sown outside in spring in milder areas, or in a greenhouse or on a windowsill. Best sown as three seeds to a section in polystyrene trays; thin out to strongest seedling. Maintain a temperature of 61°F (16°C). Germination is variable. It may be necessary to nip out the tip of the seedling to prevent lanky growth. Harden off, and plant out in rows 1½ft (45cm) apart, leaving 1ft (30cm) between plants. A sunny position in well-drained soil is preferred. Foliar feed weekly with a soluble fertilizer high in potash for good blooms.

Staking: Not necessary, though some plants may topple over, in which case prop up with a twig.
Pests and diseases: Usually trouble free.
When to cut: There are two options. Either pick the small stems as the first flowers open, as these are useful in small arrangements; or wait until most of the flowers are open and there are still a few buds and then pick the whole stem. Some of the top flowers may be overblown, but you can easily nip these off. The first method is fiddly, the second much easier.
Drying: Bunch according to size and hang upside down to dry. Heat is not necessary, but a warm room is required.
Drying time: 8–10 days.
Arranging: Useful in all arrangements.

LEFT: *Helipterum manglesii*

Limonium STATICE

L. sinuatum (HH) Mediterranean
Height: 1–2½ft (30–75cm)
Colour: All shades

How to grow: Sow in seed trays in a greenhouse or on a windowsill. Maintain a temperature of 55–61°F (13–16°C). Germination is usually very good, so half trays may be adequate. Prick out into sectioned trays, harden off and plant out when all danger of frosts has passed in rows 1½ft (45cm) apart, leaving 1ft (30cm) between plants. Statice can be a difficult plant to grow. It needs good soil, shelter, plenty of sun, and weekly feeds of liquid fertilizer. Tomato fertilizer is good, as is a foliar feed high in potash. In bad summers, and in colder areas, you will be at the mercy of the weather. Only the purple, blue, and white varieties seem to do really well; the pink are variable, and the yellow and apricot do not always produce good

Limonium sinuatum

heads. In a very mild winter, the plants may survive to flower again, but the blooms may not be of good quality.

Staking: Not necessary.
Pests and diseases: Usually trouble free.
When to cut: When the whole of the flower head is open.
Drying: Bunch together 5–10 stems and hang upside down to dry.
Drying time: 5–10 days.
Arranging: A most useful filler.

Limonium

L. suworowii (Pink pokers)
(HH) W Turkestan
Height: 1–2½ft (30–75cm)
Colour: Pink/red

How to grow: Sow in half trays in a greenhouse or on a windowsill. Germination is usually excellent. Maintain a temperature of 65–70°F (18–21°C). Prick out into sectioned trays, harden off and plant out when all danger of frosts has passed, leaving 1ft (30cm) between plants and 1½ft (45cm) between rows. Well-drained soil and a sunny position is preferred. Foliar feed weekly.

Staking: Not necessary.
Pests and diseases: Usually trouble free.
When to cut: When about half the stem has open flowers, it is ready to pick. Do not leave too long.
Drying: Bunch together 8–12 stems and hang upside down to dry. Some heat is helpful.
Drying time: 1–2 weeks.
Arranging: Useful for outlines.

Linum FLAX

L. usitatissimum (H) SW Asia
Height: 1½–2½ft (45–75cm)
Colour: Seed heads green, turning to
brown when ripe

How to grow: This plant is a delight
with its bright blue flowers, but it is
also grown for its seed heads. Sow
outside in early spring. Germination is
very good. Thin out seedlings to
10–12in (25–30cm). It is tricky to pick,
as the heads get tangled together, so
space well apart in a sunny position.
Feeding is not usually needed.

Staking: May need string and bamboos
if growth is vigorous.
Pests and diseases: Can be attacked by
aphids. Spray with an insecticide of
your choice.
When to cut: When the seed heads are
still green.
Drying: It is best to hang up sprays
individually if you are only growing a
few plants; on a larger scale, only
bunch a few sprays together at a time,
as the heads can tangle. Heat is not
necessary.
Drying time: 1–2 weeks.
Arranging: Useful in all arrangements,
but care is needed to prevent the heads
getting caught up on other flowers.

Lonas

L. inodora (H) SW Mediterranean
Height: 1–1½ft (30–45cm)
Colour: Yellow

How to grow: Sow outside in rows in early spring. Well-drained soil in a sunny position preferred. Thin out to 10–12in (25–30cm) apart. Foliar feed weekly. This plant is like a small achillea, and can be useful, though rather tiresome to pick with its many side stems.

Staking: Not necessary.
Pests and diseases: Usually trouble free.
When to cut: When the heads are fully formed, but before they start to turn brown.
Drying: Bunch together 10–12 stems and hang upside down to dry.
Drying time: 1–2 weeks.
Arranging: Useful in all arrangements.

Lonas inodora

Moluccella
BELLS OF IRELAND

M. laevis (H) W Asia
Height: 1½–2½ft (45–75cm)
Colour: Green turning to cream
when dry

How to grow: Sow in seed trays in a
greenhouse or on a windowsill, or sow
three seeds to a sectioned tray,
thinning out to strongest seedling. The
seeds can take some time to germinate,
and this can be variable. Harden off
and plant out when safe to do so in
good, well-drained soil, in a sunny
position. Plant in rows, leaving 1ft
(30cm) between plants and 1½ft
(45cm) between rows. Foliar feed.

Staking: Not necessary, but some
support may be helpful if the plants
grow very tall.
Pests and diseases: Usually trouble
free.
When to cut: Not before the tiny white
flowers open in the bracts.
Drying: Pick off all the leaves, and nip
off the top two or three small bracts, as
these will not dry well. Hang upside
down to dry over a boiler or in an
airing cupboard for a few days, and
then keep in a warm room. Although
preserving in glycerine solution is an
option, moluccella frequently goes
limp and sticky. They dry perfectly well
by the air method, and are very long
lasting.
Drying time: 1–3 weeks.
Arranging: Lovely in large
arrangements.

Nigella LOVE-IN-A-MIST

N. damascena (H) Mediterranean,
S Europe and Middle East
Height: 1½–2ft (45–60cm)
Colour: Green/purple seed heads

How to grow: Sow outside in spring in
a sunny position, in well-drained soil.
Leave 1½ft (45cm) between rows and
thin out seedlings to 8–12in (20–30cm)
between plants. Germination is usually

good. Foliar feed weekly. Take off some of the smaller side buds to encourage good-sized heads. The flowers do not dry, but are grown for their attractive seed heads, which are green, sometimes shaded with purple.

Staking: This may be necessary if the flowers grow very tall. Use bamboos and string if they are planted in rows; individual plants can be supported with a strong twig.

Pests and diseases: Usually trouble free.
When to cut: When the seed heads are fully formed, but before they start to turn brown, or the weather spoils them.
Drying: Strip off the lower leaves, bunch together 10–15 stems and hang upside down to dry.
Drying time: 1–2 weeks.
Arranging: Useful in small and medium-sized arrangements.

Nigella damascena

Papaver POPPY

P. somniferum (H) S Europe and
W Asia
Cultivars 'Pink Chiffon', 'Hen and
Chickens', and *P. giganticum*
Height: 1½–3ft (45–90cm)
Colour: Green/brown seed heads

How to grow: Once you have grown
'Pink Chiffon' it will seed itself, and
can become a nuisance, but it is easily
removed, though it does not
transplant. Sow in rows in early spring,
and thin out to 1–1½ft (30–45cm)
apart, leaving 1½ft (45cm) between
rows. Any soil and almost any position
is suitable. This plant is grown for its
seed pods; the flowers do not dry.

Staking: Not necessary.
Pests and diseases: Usually trouble
free.

When to cut: As soon as the seed
heads are well formed and feel firm
when pressed. Do not leave them too
long, as they get spoilt by bad weather
and frosts. Success depends very much
on the year; a cold, wet summer will
not allow the pods to mature in time,
but hot, dry summers produce
excellent results. 'Pink Chiffon' is
a good variety, and the amusing
'Hen and Chickens' has tiny 'babies'
around the base of the pod, though
not all heads will produce these.
P. giganticum, as its name implies,
produces huge seed heads.
Drying: Strip off the leaves, and bunch
together 10–15 stems and hang to dry.
The pods are like pepper-pots, and
when dry the seeds will shake out.
Drying time: 1–3 weeks.
Arranging: Useful in all but the
smallest arrangements; effective
sprayed gold or silver at Christmas.

1 *Papaver somniferum*
'Pink Chiffon'; **2** *Papaver
somniferum* 'Hen and
Chickens'; **3** *Papaver
gigantioum.*

RIGHT: *Papaver
somniferum
'Pink Chiffon'*

Xeranthemum
HARRISONIA

X. annuum (HH) Mediterranean and Orient
Height: 1½–2½ft (45–75cm)
Colour: Purple, pink and white

How to grow: Sow outside in double rows 1ft (30cm) apart in late spring. Thin out to 9–12in (22.5–30cm) between seedlings. Well-drained soil and a sunny position preferred. Foliar feed weekly. In poor summers, these flowers can be rather late in coming into flower, so it is worth getting a good start by using expanding cloches.

Staking: Yes. Nets and bamboos.
Pests and diseases: Usually trouble free.
When to cut: As soon as the flowers are fully open, though this is one of the few dried flowers that can be left for a few days when ready.
Drying: Bunch together 15–20 stems and hang upside down to dry.
Drying time: 1–2 weeks.
Arranging: Useful in all arrangements. They have good, strong stems.

Xeranthemum annuum

PERENNIALS

Acanthus mollis

Acanthus
BEAR'S BREECHES

A. mollis (FH) Italy
Height: 3ft (90cm)
Colour: Cream and purple flowers

A. spinosus (H) SE Europe
Height: 3–4ft (90–120cm)
Colour: Cream and purple flowers

How to grow: A handsome perennial plant with tall spikes of purple and cream flowers. The leaves have been the inspiration for much fine carving. *A. mollis* flowers well in milder areas, but *A. spinosus* is recommended for cooler climates, though can be delayed by very cold winters in coming into growth in the spring, and the flowers and picking time will be later. Most good nurseries stock the large, fleshy roots. It can also be grown from seed. The clumps become very large, so allow 2–3ft (60–90cm) between them. Feed with Blood, Fish and Bone, or general purpose fertilizer. Plant in good rich soil, in a sunny position.

Staking: Not usually necessary, but summer gales can topple the spikes.
Pests and diseases: Usually trouble free.
When to cut: Late summer and with great care! The spikes have large thorns beneath each flower, so wear gloves. Like delphiniums, pick when all but the top 3 or 4 florets are open.
Drying: Hang individual stems upside down in airing cupboard or above boiler.
Drying time: 1–2 weeks.
Arranging: Suitable only for large arrangements.

Achillea YARROW

A. filipendulina (H) Caucasus
Height: 3–5ft (90–150cm)
Colour: Yellow/gold
Varieties: 'Cloth of Gold', 'Gold Plate', 'Coronation Gold'

Hybrid *A. clypeolata* × *A. taygetea*
Height: 1½–2ft (45–60cm)
Colour: Pale yellow
Varieties: 'Moonshine'

How to grow: A well-known herbaceous plant, with tall, strong stems and flat, yellow heads. Obtainable from nurseries, or friends will give you off-sets when dividing their clumps, which should be done every 3 or 4 years. It is easily grown from seed. It has an irritating tendency to attract couch grass, and this is best dealt with by using a weed glove. Plant in autumn or spring in a sunny position in a good, rich soil with good drainage. Allow 1½–2ft (45–60cm) between clumps. Feed with Blood, Fish and Bone, or general purpose fertilizer.

Staking: In borders, use herbaceous supports. In rows, use strong bamboos, or stakes, and strong twine.
Pests and diseases: Can be attacked by aphids. Spray with insecticide of your choice.
When to cut: Late summer, when the heads are fully mature, but before they start to go brown. You will know if you have picked too soon, as the heads will shrivel and lose colour when dried.
Drying: Strip off leaves and bunch together 5–7 stems; hang upside down to dry. Heat not necessary.
Drying time: 1–2 weeks.

1 *Achillea filipendulina;*
2 *Achillea clypeolata* ×
A. taygetea 'Moonshine'.

LEFT: *Achillea*
filipendulina
'Gold Plate'

KEY FOR PERENNIALS

(FH) = Frost hardy:
withstands temperatures
down to 23°F (−5°C)
(H) = Fully hardy:
withstands temperatures
down to 5°F (−15°C)

Arranging: Achillea is a most useful plant with heads of all sizes. The larger ones can be cut into sections and, having strong stems, are invaluable for use in cones, balls and small arrangements, making a good filler. The stems make excellent extenders. Some books recommend 'The Pearl' and 'Cerise Queen' for drying, but these do not dry particularly well.

Alchemilla
LADY'S MANTLE

A. mollis (H) Asia Minor
Height: 1½–2ft (45–60cm)
Colour: Lime green/yellow

How to grow: The well-known 'flower arranger's delight'. Feathery heads of lime green turning yellow. There are no problems with this plant, which rapidly becomes the 'gardener's nightmare' as it seeds itself everywhere. Most nurseries stock it, and friends (and enemies!) will be only too happy to give you plantlets. Plant in spring or autumn, in good, well-drained soil in a sunny position. It is usually not necessary to feed, but use Blood, Fish and Bone or a general purpose fertilizer if required. Leave plenty of room between clumps, as a plantlet will grow rapidly in one season, and it is tenacious and difficult to dig up. Keep under control by dead-heading, and renew clumps every 3–4 years.

Alchemilla mollis

Staking: Not necessary, though heavy rain can knock the flowers down.
Pests and diseases: Usually trouble free.
When to cut: One of the first flowers to pick, usually early summer. Pick either when still young and green, or a little later when the heads are starting to turn yellow and fluffy. Do not leave too long, or the heads will start to go brown.
Drying: Strip off leaves, bunch together 10–12 stems and hang upside down to dry. Heat not necessary.
Drying time: 7–10 days.
Arranging: Alchemilla is invaluable a a substitute for gypsophila, fresh or dried. Useful in all arrangements.

Anaphalis
PEARLY EVERLASTING

A. triplinervis (H) Himalayas
Height: 1ft (30cm)
Colour: White

A. yedoensis (H) Japan
Height: 2–3ft (60–90cm)
Colour: White

How to grow: A herbaceous plant with white, fluffy heads. Most nurseries stock it, or friends will give you off-sets, as it spreads rapidly and needs controlling. Chop around clumps each year to keep them within bounds, and renew clumps using off-sets every 3–4 years. Prefers ordinary, well-drained soil, in a sunny position. Feeding is not usually necessary. *A. yedoensis* is a survivor; it was one of the first plants to re-establish itself on Mount St Helen's after the volcanic eruption of 1980.

Staking: Either herbaceous supports in borders, or stakes and twine in rows.
Pests and diseases: Usually trouble free.
When to cut: Mid-summer, before the heads become too fluffy and untidy.
Drying: Strip off leaves, bunch together 10–15 stems and hang upside down to dry over boiler or in airing cupboard. Damp is fatal, and it will go limp immediately if not kept in a warm room.
Drying time: 2–3 weeks.
Arranging: A rather disappointing plant. Useful as a filler, but the heads have a tendency to flop when dry.

1 *Anaphalis triplinervis;*
2 *Anaphalis yedoensis.*

1 *Cynara cardunculus;*
2 *Cynara scolymus.*

Artichoke

Cynara scolymus (Globe artichoke)
(H) Europe
Height: 2–5ft (60–150cm)
Colour: Green, with purple flower
heads if left to open

Cynara cardunculus (Cardoon) (H)
Europe
Height: 2–6ft (60–180cm)
Colour: Green

How to grow: Either from seed, or obtain roots from nurseries or friends. Plant in good, rich soil in a sheltered position. The globe (edible) artichoke has large green heads with purple flowers, and the cardoon has smaller, similar heads. Allow plenty of space between plants – 2–4ft (60–120cm) – as the clumps grow very large, and renew every 3–4 years with off-sets, or from seed. Feed with Blood, Fish and Bone or a general fertilizer, and potash if necessary to encourage good heads.

Staking: Not usually necessary for globe artichokes, but cardoons may need support if they grow very tall.
Pests and diseases: Usually trouble free.
When to cut: Usually mid- to late summer when the purple flowers are well formed. These last for up to a year, and can then be pulled out gently leaving the beige centre underneath. The heads can be picked before the purple flowers appear, but being under-ripe may not dry well.
Drying: Hang stems upside down individually, as they are heavy. Some heat is helpful.
Drying time: 2–3 weeks.
Arranging: Only suitable for large arrangements. The heads can be sprayed gold or silver for Christmas decorations.

RIGHT: *Cynara scolymus* growing with *Eryngium giganteum.*

84

Astilbe

Hybrids (H) China/Japan
Height: 1–2ft (30–60cm)
Colour: All shades from white to pink
and red

How to grow: The feathery plumes of
astilbe come in a large range of colours
and most dry well. All good nurseries
stock them, and friends will give you
off-sets. These plants will tolerate semi-
shade, and need good, rich soil with
plenty of humus to retain moisture.
They do particularly well in bog
gardens and round pools. Plant in
spring or autumn and allow 1½–2ft
(45–60cm) between clumps as they
spread quite rapidly. Feed with Blood,
Fish and Bone or general fertilizer and
mulch well in spring to conserve
moisture. In dry summers, you will
need to water them regularly.

Staking: Not necessary.
Pests and diseases: Usually trouble
free.
When to cut: As soon as the heads are
fully formed but before they become
too fluffy.
Drying: Remove leaves, bunch
together 6–8 stems and hang upside
down. Dry quickly over a boiler or in
an airing cupboard. The dark red
varieties dry particularly well.
Drying time: 5–10 days.
Arranging: Astilbes make excellent
outliners and fillers.

RIGHT: The feathery plumes
of astilbe.

Astrantia MASTERWORT

A. maxima, syn. *A. helleborifolia*
(H) East Caucasus
Height: 1½–2½ft (45–75cm)
Colour: Pink

How to grow: A charming plant, with pin-cushion-like flowers from early to mid-summer. It is obtainable from most nurseries, or friends will give you off-sets or self-sown seedlings. Plant in borders or in rows and allow 1–2ft (30–60cm) between clumps, which will increase quite quickly. A sunny position with good, well-drained soil is preferred. Feed if necessary with Blood, Fish and Bone or a general purpose fertilizer.

Staking: Not necessary.
Pests and diseases: Usually trouble free.
When to cut: As soon as the flowers are fully formed, usually early summer.
Drying: Strip off leaves, bunch together 10–15 stems and hang upside down to dry. Heat not necessary.
Drying time: 7–10 days.
Arranging: Useful in all arrangements.

Astrantia maxima provides a backdrop for *Eryngium alpinum.*

Carlina

C. acaulis var. *caulescens* (H) Europe
Height: 10–18in (25–45cm)
Colour: Beige

How to grow: An uncommon and striking plant. Some specialist nurseries supply them but they are moderately easy to grow from fresh seed. The wild carlina has little or no stem, but the variety *C. caulescens* has stems of varying length, some reaching 1½ft (45cm) in height. Sow indoors, harden off and plant out in border or in rows 1½ft (45cm) apart. Some may flower the following year, but usually they do not flower until their second year. A good, rich soil, well-drained, sunny position is preferred. Feed with Blood, Fish and Bone, or general purpose fertilizer.

Staking: Not necessary.
Pests and diseases: Usually trouble free. Some plants can die off in very wet or very cold winters, or after 5–6 years through old age.

When to cut: With gloves! These plants have thistle-like leaves, with tiny thorns that work their way under the skin. Choose a sunny day when the heads are half to fully open. Like helichrysums they will go on opening as they dry, and can look overblown. Sizes of head vary from small to large: some can reach 5in (12.5cm) across; stems vary from 3–18in (7.5–45cm). Bees love this plant, and gather in large numbers on the open heads, where they become drowsy and, sadly, they often die.
Drying: Cut off the lower leaves, but leave a rosette round the heads. The petals are delicate, so be careful not to break them. Bunch together 3–5 stems and hang upside down to dry in a warm room, but not over direct heat, or the heads will open too far.
Drying time: 1–2 weeks.
Arranging: This is a wonderful flower for all arrangements, as the heads last for years if care is taken not to break the petals. If the stems are very short, you can insert a strong wire to give added length.

Carlina acaulis and
Limonium tataricum
(dumosa) growing in rows.

Catananche
CUPID'S DART

C. caerulea (H) Mediterranean
Height: 1½–2ft (45–60cm)
Colour: Silvery white

How to grow: This plant is grown for its silvery-white seed heads. It is obtainable from nurseries, and can be grown easily from seed. It tolerates poor soil and prefers a sunny position. Plant in borders or in rows, allowing 1½ft (45cm) between plants.

Staking: Yes; it tends to flop in late summer. Use herbaceous supports, or bamboos and string in rows.

Pests and diseases: Usually trouble free. It does have a tendency to die off in wet winters, and it resents disturbance in the autumn, so only move in spring, especially when dividing clumps.

When to cut: Some books will tell you that the blue flowers dry. They do not! The seed heads are ready in late summer.

Drying: Any remaining petals can be pulled out gently. Bunch together 24–35 stems and hang to dry. Heat not necessary.

Drying time: 5–10 days.

Arranging: Useful in swags, balls, and small arrangements.

Centaurea

C. macrocephala (H) Caucasus
Height: 3–5ft (90–150cm)
Colour: Yellow/orange

How to grow: A handsome flower of the cornflower family, which looks like a large, yellow thistle. Some nurseries supply it, but it is easily grown from seed. It takes 2–3 years before it flowers, but it is well worth the wait. The plants grow tall, but can be planted fairly close together. Allow 2ft (60cm) between rows. Good, rich soil in a sunny position preferred. Feed with Blood, Fish and Bone, or general purpose fertilizer.

Staking: Usually yes, if they grow tall. Herbaceous supports in border, or strong twine and posts in rows.
Pests and diseases: Usually trouble free, but can be attacked by aphids. Spray with insecticide of your choice.
When to cut: As soon as the yellow flowers are open, usually mid-summer, but do not leave too long, as they do not dry well when fully open. Check every day.
Drying: Strip off the leaves, bunch together 5–7 stems and hang upside down to dry over a boiler or in an airing cupboard for 2–3 days, and then in a warm room.
Drying time: 2–3 weeks.
Arranging: Good, strong stems; useful in medium-sized to large arrangements.

Centaurea macrocephala

Cirsium

C. japonicum (H) Japan
Height: 1½–2½ft (45–75cm)
Colour: Pink and red

How to grow: This is a herbaceous
'thistle'. Though it can be obtained
from nurseries, it is easy to grow from
seed, but will not flower until the
following year. It can die off in wet
winters. Reasonably good soil, well-
drained and sunny position. Feed with
Blood, Fish and Bone, or general
purpose fertilizer. Allow 1ft (30cm)
between plants in border and in rows.

Staking: Yes, if the plants grow tall.
Herbaceous supports, or bamboos and
string.
Pests and diseases: Usually trouble
free.
When to cut: As soon as the flowers
are fully formed, from early summer
onwards.
Drying: Strip off leaves, bunch
together 10–15 stems and hang upside
down to dry. Heat not necessary.
Drying time: 1–2 weeks
Arranging: Charming and long lasting
as a cut flower, and one that dries well,
though the colour of the red ones
darkens. It is useful in all
arrangements.

Delphinium

Hybrids (H)
Height: 3–7ft (90–210cm)
Colour: All shades, white to purple

How to grow: Obtainable from most nurseries, and easy to grow from seed, or from cuttings. Sow seeds in spring in a cold frame; plant out in permanent positions in late summer. In cold areas leave the plants in the cold frame until the following spring, when danger of frost has passed. Plant in border or in rows, 1½–2½ft (45–75cm) apart. Rich soil in a sunny position. Feed with Blood, Fish and Bone, or general purpose fertilizer; mulch well in spring with compost or well-rotted manure.

Staking: Yes. The tall varieties need bamboos and string, the shorter ones herbaceous supports.
Pests and diseases: Can be affected by crown rot, but usually trouble free.
When to cut: When all but the top two or three florets are open. The very large Pacific hybrids and the charming Belladonna hybrids do not dry well.
Drying: Strip off the leaves and hang individually upside down in the airing cupboard or over the boiler. Dry as quickly as possible. I find only the blue ones dry really well; the white and pink varieties tend to discolour.
Drying time: 5–10 days.
Arranging: Excellent for medium-sized to very large arrangements.

LEFT: Delphiniums in the border.

1 *Dipsacus sylvestris;*
2 *Dipsacus fullonum.*

Dipsacus   TEASEL

D. sylvestris (Common teasel) (H)
Europe and Asia
Height: 3–6ft (90–180cm)
Colour: Green/beige/brown according
to when picked

D. fullonum (Fuller's teasel) (H)
Europe and Asia
Height: 2–3ft (60–90cm)
Colour: Beige/brown according to
when picked

How to grow: *D. sylvestris* is the
common teasel of wild ground and *D.
fullonum* is the cultivated variety used
for carding cloth; it has larger, stronger
hooks than the wild teasel. *D.
sylvestris* grows in the wild, and seeds
collected will grow almost anywhere.
Seeds of both can be bought. They are
bi-annuals. Sow in autumn or spring in
a seed bed and transplant to rows, or
wild ground if you want the plants to
naturalize. They will produce heads the
following year. Goldfinches love this
plant and come for the seeds in the
autumn and winter, so try to leave
some heads for them, and for re-
seeding. Feeding is not necessary.

Staking: Gales can topple very tall
plants, otherwise staking is not
necessary.
Pests and diseases: Trouble free.
When to cut: A matter of personal
preference, usually ready late summer,
or early autumn. Do not pick too early,
although the heads are most attractive
while still green, they will not dry well.
The purple flowers among the hooks
will fade and die, and can be brushed
out using another teasel when fully dry.

Somewhere between beige and brown
is best. They get dark and too
weathered if left too long.
Drying: Use gloves! Strip off leaves,
bunch together 5–7 stems and hang
upside down to dry. Heat is not
necessary.
Drying time: 1–3 weeks, depending
when picked.
Arrangements: Useful for medium-
sized to large arrangements. A light
coating of gold spray brightens any that
have gone too dark, and a thicker
coating makes them useful for
Christmas decorations, with sprayed
poppy heads and artichokes.

Echinops GLOBE THISTLE

E. ritro (H) Europe and W Asia
Height: 3–5ft (90–150cm)
Colour: Slate blue

E. sphaerocephalus (H) W Asia
Height: 4–6ft (120–180cm)
Colour: Grey/green

How to grow: A tall herbaceous plant, with round spiky heads. *E. ritro* is obtainable from most nurseries, or friends will give you roots when dividing the clumps. These get very large and need lifting and dividing every 4–5 years, replanting only the young, outer shoots. The roots, like those of eryngium and acanthus, go down a very long way, and care is needed not to break them, as any pieces left will re-grow. *E. sphaerocephalus* is not easy to find, but is worth hunting down. The heads last for years and do not shatter like *E. ritro*. Good, rich soil, and a sunny position is preferred. Feed if necessary with Blood, Fish and Bone or general purpose fertilizer.

Staking: Yes. Large, strong herbaceous supports, or posts and twine if in rows.
Pests and diseases: Often attacked by aphids. Watch carefully as these can ruin the emerging heads. Spray with an insecticide of your choice.
When to cut: Picked before the blue flowers appear, but when the heads are well formed and have a good colour ('Taplow Blue' is a good variety), they dry well. (Picked after the flowers appear, the heads shatter when dry.)
Drying: Use gloves. Strip off the leaves, bunch together 10–15 stems and hang upside down to dry. Heat is not necessary, but a warm room is helpful. When the heads are dry, a squirt of hair spray can help to stop them from shattering. Handle with care, as they are a little brittle.
Drying time: 1–2 weeks.
Arranging: Useful in all arrangements.

1 *Echinops ritro;*
2 *Echinops sphaerocephalus.*

Echinops ritro with *Achillea anthea.*

Eryngium

All the four eryngiums listed are the 'superstars' of the dried flower grower's garden. As they are so attractive, you may not want to remove them from the border when they are ready, so plant some in a cutting row where they will not be missed when the time comes to pick them for drying.

E. alpinum (H) Europe
Height: 2–4ft (60–120cm)
Colour: Electric blue

How to grow: This is a beautiful plant with large, electric-blue heads. It is obtainable from some nurseries, or they can be grown from fresh seed. Good, rich soil, with good drainage, and a sunny position is preferred. Leave 1½–2ft (45–60cm) between plants. Feed with Blood, Fish and Bone or general purpose fertilizer.

Staking: Yes. Herbaceous supports.
Pests and diseases: Usually trouble free.
When to cut: When the heads are fully formed and of a good colour, usually mid-summer.
Drying: Strip off lower leaves, bunch together not more than 3 heads, and hang upside down to dry for 3–5 days. If you can then stand them upright in a tall container that will support the heads until they are fully dry, it will prevent the heads from closing up too much. Heat is not necessary, but a warm room is helpful.
Drying time: Probably 1–2 weeks.
Arranging: Beautiful in medium-sized to large arrangements, and the heads last for many years.

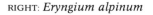
RIGHT: *Eryngium alpinum*

Eryngium

E. × oliverianum (H)
Height: 2–3ft (60–90cm)
Colour: Grey/blue

How to grow: As for *E. alpinum.*
The heads are paler in colour and are
more open.

Staking: Yes. Herbaceous supports.
Pests and diseases: Usually trouble
free.
When to cut: Usually ready early to
mid-summer. Cut when the heads are
fully formed and of good colour, but
do not allow to turn brown.
Drying: Strip off lower leaves, bunch
together 3–5 stems and hang upside
down. Heat is not necessary, but a
warm room is helpful.
Drying time: 1–2 weeks.
Arranging: Useful in medium-sized to
large arrangements.

Eryngium

E. giganteum (Miss Willmott's ghost)
(H) Caucasus. Biennial
Height: 2–4ft (60–120cm)
Colour: Silvery grey/green

How to grow: This is a wonderful plant, with very strong sprays of (sharp!) heads. There is a charming story about it which concerns the Edwardian lady gardener, Miss Willmott. She kept seed in her pocket and used to sprinkle this surreptiously in the borders when visiting other gardens. When the owners found young plants appearing in due course, they would say 'Miss Willmott has been here', hence the name, Miss Willmott's ghost. Some nurseries stock the plant, or friends will give you self-sown seedlings or fresh seeds. Good, rich soil, with good drainage and a sunny position is preferred. Leave 1–1½ft (30–45cm) between plants. Feed with Blood, Fish and Bone, or general purpose fertilizer.

Staking: Yes; herbaceous supports, or posts and twine if in rows.
Pests and diseases: Usually trouble free.

When to cut: Ready usually in mid- to late summer. The main head will be ready first, so cut this (use gloves) and then wait until the rest of the spray is ripe. Do not allow the heads to turn brown, but leave some heads to go to seed for self- or re-sowing.
Drying: Insert a strong wire in the main heads, and hang upside down to dry. For the sprays, bunch together 3–5 and hang upside down to dry. Heat is not necessary, but a warm room is helpful.
Drying time: Variable, usually 1–2 weeks.
Arranging: A wonderful plant for all arrangements, as the heads differ in size and last for many years.

Eryngium giganteum

96

Eryngium

E. planum and *E. tripartitum*
(H) E Europe
Height: 2–4ft (50–120cm)
Colour: Blue/green. These two plants are almost indistinguishable; there is a slight difference in the leaves.

How to grow: Obtainable from good nurseries, or friends will give you young plants, as they increase rapidly. They prefer good, rich soil, good drainage, and a sunny position. Feed with Blood, Fish and Bone, or general purpose fertilizer.

Staking: Yes. Herbaceous supports, or twine and posts if grown in rows.

Pests and diseases: Usually trouble free.

When to cut: When the little heads start to turn blue, which is usually in mid- to late summer. Do not wait until all the heads on the sprays have got colour, or the larger ones will become overripe.

Drying: Strip off the leaves, bunch together 6–12 stems and hang upside down to dry. Heat is not necessary but a warm room is helpful.

Drying time: 1–2 weeks.

Arranging: A most useful plant, as you can cut off individual heads and use them in small arrangements, or use the whole spray in large displays.

Eryngium tripartitum

LEFT: *Eryngium tripartitum*

97

Gnaphalium

G. var. 'Fairy Gold' (H) Europe
Height: 1–1½ft (30–45cm)
Colour: Pale lemon to orange

Helichrysum var. 'Sulphur Light'
(H) SW Europe
Height: 1–2ft (30–60cm)
Colour: Yellow

I have grouped these two plants together because they are almost indistinguishable.

How to grow: Helichrysum is obtainable at nurseries; gnaphalium is easy to grow from seed. Do not cover the seeds as they need light to germinate; keep the temperature between 60–70°F (16–21°C). Plant 1ft (30cm) apart. A sunny position and well-drained soil; these plants dislike excessive moisture. Feed with Blood, Fish and Bone if necessary.

Staking: Not necessary.
Pests and Diseases: They can be attacked by aphids. Spray with insecticide. If you are prey to rabbits in your garden, protect these plants with netting in the winter, as rabbits find gnaphalium irresistible.
When to cut: As soon as the flowers are well formed, but before they start to go brown. The strong curry smell of gnaphalium can be overwhelming when stripping the leaves.
Drying: Bunch together 10–12 stems and hang to dry. Heat is helpful.
Drying time: 2–3 weeks.
Arranging: Useful for all arrangements.

Gnaphalium 'Fairy Gold'

Gypsophila

G. paniculata (H) E Europe
Height: 2–3ft (60–90cm)
Colour: White
Varieties: 'Bristol Fairy', 'Baby's Breath'

How to grow: A charming plant, with tiny white flowers in late summer. The long tap root can be bought from nurseries. 'Baby's Breath' has single flowers, while 'Bristol Fairy' has larger, double flowers. It needs to be planted 2ft (60cm) apart, as it grows into a large clump in time. Good soil, with good drainage and a sunny position is preferred. Mulch with compost in spring and, if necessary, feed with Blood, Fish and Bone or general purpose fertilizer.

Staking: Not usually necessary.
Pests and diseases: Usually trouble free.
When to cut: When the tiny flowers are beginning to open. Do not leave too late, as they spoil easily in bad weather and the flowers can shrivel. Care is needed when picking, as the heads get tangled together and can break.
Drying: Hang upside down in individual sprays. Heat is not necessary.
Drying time: 5–10 days.
Arranging: A delightful finishing touch to all arrangements, making them look as though edged with fine lace.

1 *Gypsophila paniculata* 'Bristol Fairy';
2 *Gypsophila paniculata* 'Baby's Breath'.

Gypsophila paniculata 'Bristol Fairy'

Helichrysum

H. acuminatum (FH) New Zealand
Height: 6–12in (15–30cm)
Colour: Golden yellow

How to grow: This is a small perennial helichrysum which resembles the annual *H. bracteatum*. It is not easy to find, but can be grown from seed. In a small garden it can be useful, but is not recommended for growing on a large scale. It requires a sunny position and good, well-drained soil. Feeding is not usually necessary.

Staking: Not necessary.
Pests and diseases: Usually trouble free.
When to pick: When the flowers are just beginning to open.
Drying: The stems are strong, so there is no need to wire them. Bunch together 8–10 and hang to dry.
Drying time: 5–10 days.
Arranging: Useful in small and medium-sized arrangements.

Hydrangea

H. macrophylla, syn. *H. hortensis* (FH) China and Japan
Height: 4–10ft (120–300cm)
Colour: Blue, pink and green/blue, depending on the soil

How to grow: A shrub that should be planted in autumn in good loamy soil, adding compost and peat. It needs plenty of moisture. Do not plant where the new buds can be damaged by early

morning sun after frosts. They tolerate semi-shade or full sun. On alkaline soil, the flowers will be pink; on acid, blue. An annual mulch of well-rotted manure is beneficial.

Staking: Not necessary.
Pests and diseases: Usually trouble free, but aphids can attack stems and foliage. Yellowing of the leaves denotes chlorosis, so treat with sequestrene.
When to cut: In early autumn, when the flower heads feel slightly papery.

Do not cut the stems too long, or you may remove the next year's buds.
Drying: Much depends on the bush for the quality of drying. Some bushes seem to produce flowers that dry better than others. The best method is to stand the stems in 2in (5cm) of water and leave till this is absorbed and the heads are dry.
Drying time: Times vary greatly, usually from 2–4 weeks.
Arranging: Useful in medium-sized to large arrangements.

LEFT: *Hydrangea macrophylla*

Liatris
BLAZING STAR, GAYFEATHER

L. spicata (H) USA
Height: 2–3ft (60–90cm)
Colour: Pink, purple

How to grow: An easily grown perennial that likes moist soil. They do well in bog gardens. Easily obtained from most nurseries, and can be grown from seed. Plant 1–1½ft (30–45cm) apart, and feed with Blood, Fish and Bone. Mulch well in spring.

Staking: Not necessary.
Pests and diseases: Usually trouble free.
When to cut: When the heads are fully formed, but before they become too fluffy.
Drying: Bunch together 6–8 stems and hang to dry. Heat is not necessary, but a warm room is helpful.
Drying time: 1–2 weeks.
Arranging: Useful for giving height and emphasis to outline in medium-sized to large arrangements.

Limonium

L. latifolium (H) E Europe and S Russia
Height: 1½–2½ft (45–75cm)
Colour: Blue

L. tataricum (H) (Dumosa)
Height: 1–2ft (30–60cm)
Colour: White

How to grow: *L. latifolium* is obtainable from some nurseries, but dumosa is not easy to find. Fortunately, it is easy to grow from seed, but only if this is of good quality. It has an infuriating habit of surviving hard winters only to go brown and die off in early summer. Some plants last for years, others die when quite young. So

Limonium latifolium

I always grow spare plants from seed each year. Harden off and plant outside in rows 1–1½ft (30–45cm) apart, and 1ft (30cm) between plants. Good soil, with good drainage and a sunny position. Feed with Blood, Fish and Bone, or general purpose fertilizer. Extra potash in spring can be helpful, as can an occasional foliar feed.

Staking: Not necessary.
Pests and diseases: Usually trouble free.
When to cut: Cut *L. latifolium* when the tiny blue flowers are opening. Cut dumosa when the white flowers are nearly all open.
Drying: Bunch together 3–4 stems and hang to dry. Heat is not necessary, but a warm room is helpful.
Drying time: 5–10 days.
Arranging: *L. latifolium* can be used like gypsophila, and dumosa is invaluable in all arrangements. It has strong stems, and can be cut into little pieces for use in small arrangements. It is one of the most useful and versatile of all dried flowers.

1 *Limonium latifolium;*
2 *Limonium tataricum.*

Linum FLAX

L. narbonense (H) S Europe
Height: 1–2ft (30–60cm)
Colour: Green/brown seed heads.

How to grow: This perennial flax produces blue flowers each morning but, like the annual variety, is grown for its seed heads. A short-lived plant; renew from cuttings or from seed. Plant 1ft (30cm) apart in well-drained soil in spring in a sunny position. Feeding is not necessary.

Staking: Not necessary.
Pests and diseases: Usually trouble free.
When to cut: Before the seed heads turn brown and split open.
Drying: Hang the seed heads upside down in small bunches. Heat is not necessary, but a warm, airy room is helpful.
Drying time: 2–3 weeks.
Arranging: Linum is useful in all arrangements, and looks particularly effective sprayed red for Christmas decorations.

Linum narbonense

104

Lunaria HONESTY

L. annua, syn. *L. biennis* (H) Europe
Biennial
Height: 1½–2½ft (45–75cm)
Colour: Silvery white, with green or
purple outer casings

How to grow: Honesty grows very
easily! It can become quite a nuisance,
seeding itself all over the garden, but is
easily pulled out and, if still young, can
be transplanted. Sow in rows in early
summer, and then thin out to 10–12in
(25–30cm) apart. Leave 1½ft (45cm)
between rows. Being a biennial, it will
flower the following summer. It grows
in any soil, and tolerates semi-shade. It
does not need feeding.

Staking: Not necessary.
Pests and diseases: Trouble free.
When to cut: Either pick early when
the seed pods are still green, or leave
till they have changed to beige and feel
papery. Some plants produce attractive
purple seed pods, and these can be
dried as they are.
Drying: The traditional way is to pick
and bunch carefully (as the heads get
tangled) and hang up to dry. If you
delay picking too long, the pods will
start to open and go brown, staining
the silvery 'petals' inside. Once they
are dry, peel off the outer casing. They
are harder to open when picked in
good time but are well worth the effort,
as they will have a luminous, pale
green appearance which is most
attractive. They last for many years. If
you have not allowed some plants to
remain to self-sow, keep seeds for the
following year.
Drying time: 2–3 weeks.
Arranging: Can be used in many
arrangements, though it is tricky to use,
as the 'petals' are easily torn. It can be
very effective used in Christmas
decorations.

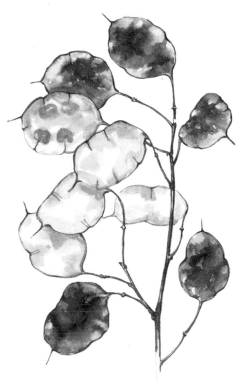

Lunaria annua

Physalis CHINESE LANTERNS, CAPE GOOSEBERRIES

P. franchetii (H) Japan
Height: 1½–2½ft (45–75cm)
Colour: Green/yellow/orange

How to grow: The long roots can be obtained from some nurseries, or friends may give you them. This plant is very invasive and has a perverse habit of flourishing where you do not want it to grow, and not where you do. Be sure to plant it where it can be contained. It can also be grown from seed, either in a cold frame or in colder areas in the greenhouse. Prick out when small and put into pots; plant out when hardened off. Any reasonable soil with full sun is preferred. Feed with Blood, Fish and Bone or general purpose fertilizer, and foliar feed for good-sized lanterns.

Staking: Not necessary.
Pests and diseases: Usually trouble free.
When to cut: When the lanterns are fully formed and starting to change colour. Unless you want them all orange, pick when only a few of the lower ones are this colour, and the others shading from green to yellow to orange down the stem. There is always a risk that bad weather will spoil the lanterns, as they tend to ripen in late summer, so do not delay picking.
Drying: Strip off leaves, bunch 5–8 stems and hang upside down to dry. Heat is not necessary, but a warm room is required.
Drying time: 1–2 weeks.
Arranging: Useful in large arrangements.

Polygonum KNOTWEED

P. affine var. 'Dimity' (H) Nepal
Height: 10–15in (25–37.5cm)
Colour: Red

P. bistorta var. 'Superbum' (H) Europe
and Asia
Height: 1½–2½ft (45–75cm)
Colour: Pink

How to grow: *P. bistorta* is an invasive
herbaceous plant, producing pink
spikes in early summer. It is obtainable
from nurseries. Off-sets are easily
broken off the parent plant, and take
well if planted at once in good soil in
borders or in rows, with 1½ft (45cm)
between plants. *P. affine* is more
invasive and makes good ground
cover, producing prolific red flowers.
Feed with Blood, Fish and Bone.

Staking: Not necessary.
Pests and diseases: Trouble free.
When to cut: One of the first flowers
you will pick, though the variety
'Dimity' will come later. Cut as soon as
the heads are fully formed, but before
they go fluffy.
Drying: Strip off leaves, bunch
together 15–20 stems and hang to dry.
Heat is not necessary.
Drying time: 5–10 days.
Arranging: Useful as outliners in
arrangements.

1 *Polygonum bistorta*
'Superbum'; 2 *Polygonum
affine* 'Dimity'.

Polygonum bistorta

107

Solidago GOLDEN ROD

S. × hybrida (H) USA
Height: 1½–4ft (45–120cm)
depending on variety
Colour: Yellow to gold

How to grow: This well-known herbaceous plant produces sprays of yellow and gold flowers in late summer. There are many varieties, but an outstanding one is called 'Lena'. This has mimosa-like heads and dries beautifully, and is not too tall. Some varieties get too fluffy and turn brown when dried. Plant in good soil in a sunny position in autumn or spring. Feed with Blood, Fish and Bone or general purpose fertilizer. Plant 'Lena' 1ft (30cm) apart, and larger varieties 1½–2ft (45–60cm) apart.

Staking: Not necessary for shorter varieties, but the taller ones will need herbaceous supports, or bamboo and string if in rows.
Pests and diseases: Usually trouble free.
When to cut: They continue to open as they dry so pick as soon as the top florets start to open. They look much nicer under- rather than over-developed.
Drying: Strip off leaves, bunch together 5–8 stems and hang upside down to dry. Heat is not necessary, but a warm room is advisable.
Drying time: 1–2 weeks.
Arranging: Useful as a filler in all arrangements.

Solidago × hybrida 'Lena'

Stachys LAMB'S EARS

S. lanata (H) Caucasus
Height: 1–1½ft (30–45cm)
Colour: Grey

How to grow: A somewhat invasive plant, with velvety leaves and spikes of grey, with tiny purple flowers. Obtainable at nurseries, or from friends as off-sets. It establishes rapidly. Any soil suitable, but a sunny position with good drainage is preferred. Feeding not usually necessary.

Staking: Not necessary.
Pests and diseases: Trouble free.
When to cut: As soon as the tiny purple flowers appear. Do not leave too long as these will go brown.
Drying: Strip only the lower leaves; bunch together 6–10 stems and hang to dry. Heat is not necessary, but a warm room is advisable.
Drying time: 2–3 weeks.
Arranging: Being grey, it is most attractive when used with blue and pink flowers. The heads can be brittle, so take care when handling them.

Stachys lanata

GRASSES

1 Briza minor; 2 Lagurus ovatus; 3 Phalaris canariensis.

Briza QUAKING GRASS

B. maxima and *B. minor* (H) S Europe
Height: 1–1½ft (30–45cm)
Colour: Green/beige

How to grow: Both large and small quaking grass are very attractive, but they are difficult to pick. The heads get tangled up and tend to snap off when you try to disentangle them. Always thin out the grass, leaving plenty of room between each clump. Sow outside in spring.

Staking: Not necessary.
Pests and diseases: Usually trouble free.
When to cut: When the heads are well formed, and of good colour.
Drying: In small bunches or as individual stems.
Drying time: 4–8 days.
Arranging: Attractive in many arrangements, but tricky to handle.

Lagurus HARE'S TAIL GRASS

L. ovatus (H) Europe
Height: 10–18in (25–45cm)
Colour: Green, fading to beige

How to grow: Sow outside in rows in spring. Well-drained soil in a sunny position is preferred. If you want very large heads, thin out when the seedlings become overcrowded. Foliar feed weekly. Germination is usually good.

Staking: Not necessary.
Pests and diseases: Can be infected with aphids. Spray with insecticide of your choice.

When to cut: When the heads are fully formed, and are proud of the leaves by about 2–3in (5–7.5cm).
Drying: Gently pull the stems, or cut them. Bunch together 20–30 and hang to dry. Heat is not necessary.
Drying time: 4–8 days.
Arranging: Useful in small and medium-sized arrangements.

Phalaris CANARY GRASS

P. canariensis (H) Europe
Height: 1–1½ft (30–45cm)
Colour: Green

How to grow: This grass can be sown outside in mild areas, but otherwise it is best to start it off in polystyrene sectioned trays. Sow three seeds, and later thin out to one seedling. Harden off and plant out when safe to do so, 4in (10cm) apart in rows. Sunny position and well-drained soil is preferred. This plant does *not* like foliar feed. If it shows signs of turning yellow this denotes magnesium deficiency. Apply Epsom salts in a solution of ¼lb to 2½ gall (100g to 1l) water.

Staking: Not usually necessary.
Pests and diseases: Can be infected with aphids. Spray with an insecticide of your choice.
When to cut: When the heads are fully formed and proud of the leaves.
Drying: Pull stalks gently, or cut them. Remove leaves and bunch together 15–25 stalks and hang to dry. Heat is not necessary.
Drying time: 5–10 days.
Arranging: Useful in small- and medium-sized arrangements.

Setaria FOXTAIL GRASS

S. glauca (H) Europe
Height: 1–2ft (30–60cm)
Colour: Green turning to yellow

How to grow: Best sown in polystyrene sectioned trays in the greenhouse, or on a windowsill. Sow three seeds and thin to one seedling. Harden off and plant out when safe to do so, 9in (22.5cm) apart, in rows. Foliar feed if necessary.

Staking: Not necessary.
Pests and diseases: Can be attacked by aphids. Spray with an insecticide of your choice.
When to cut: When the heads are fully formed and have turned yellow.
Drying: Bunch together 15–20 stalks of grass and hang to dry.
Drying time: 4–8 days.
Arranging: Useful in all arrangements.

S. macrochaeta, syn. *S. italica* (H) Europe
Height: 1–2½ft (30–75cm)
Colour: Green, turning to yellow

How to grow: Sow in rows outside in spring; protect with expanding cloche if the weather is very cold. Well-drained soil in a sunny position is preferable. Germination is variable. Thin out seedlings so they are 4–6in (10–15cm) apart. Weekly foliar feed desirable.

Staking: Not usually necessary.
Pests and diseases: Can be infected with aphids. Spray with an insecticide of your choice.

When to cut: When the heads are fully formed and turning yellow.
Drying: Strip off the long leaves, bunch together 10–15 stalks and hang to dry. Heat is not necessary.
Drying time: 5–10 days.
Arranging: Useful in medium-sized and large arrangements.

Triticum

T. spelta (H) Europe
Height: 1½–3ft (45–90cm)
Colour: Green

How to grow: This grass can be sown outside or in polystyrene sectioned trays in a greenhouse or on a windowsill. Germination is variable. Large seeds; sow one to a section. Harden off and plant out when safe to do so, leaving 6in (15cm) between plants. Foliar feed if necessary. This grass has a tendency to form large basal clumps of leaves with few stems.

Staking: Not necessary.
Pests and diseases: Can be attacked by aphids. Spray with an insecticide of your choice.
When to cut: When stems are a good length and heads are fully formed.
Drying: Bunch together 15–25 stalks and hang to dry.
Drying time: 7–10 days.
Arranging: Makes a good outliner in medium-sized and large arrangements.

PREVIOUS PAGES 110–111:
This arrangement includes Briza maxima, *oats, wheat, setaria,* Lagurus ovatus.

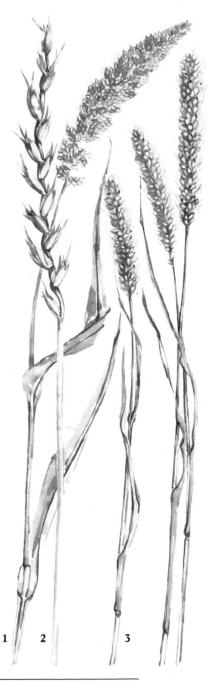

1 *Triticum spelta;* 2 *Setaria macrochaeta;*
3 *Setaria glauca.*

HERBS

1 *Marjoram;* 2 *Chive;*
3 *Lavender.*

PREVIOUS PAGES 114–115: *The plants include marjoram, tansy, curry plant, lavender, bay, bergamot, thyme, chives, lovage, sage and dill.*

Some herbs dry well, and have the added bonus of smelling delicious when used in arrangements. Details of cultivation are not given here as most of them grow easily almost anywhere, as long as they are not planted in damp and shady areas. They enjoy sun and well-drained soil, and many of them seed themselves profusely.

Pot Marjoram (H) produces quantities of self-sown seedlings. The pink flowers of this perennial are usually ready in mid- to late summer. Pick when there is a mixture of part opened and unopened flowers. Do not remove the leaves; any that need to be stripped off later at the base of the stem can be used in pot pourri. Pot marjoram makes a splendid filler, though the heads are a little brittle. The stems are very strong. Hang in bunches to dry.

Tansy (H) has tiny, yellow flowers that dry well. In cool areas this perennial tends to grow very tall, and can need staking; in warm areas it is more easily managed. Tansy is very easy to grow, though it can be a little invasive. Pick when the yellow flowers are well formed, but before they start to turn brown. Hang in bunches to dry.

Thyme (H) dries well (particularly the tall varieties) and, like pot marjoram, it has a lovely scent and will enjoy a warm, sunny position. If you have a patio or paved area, plant it between the flagstones, or in little beds, where it will flourish. Bees love thyme and pot marjoram, as do butterflies. Pick when the flower heads are well formed and of good colour, but do not leave too late. Hang in bunches to dry.

Lavender (H) is so well known it hardly needs mentioning, but not everyone appreciates the importance of picking this perennial at the right time. If you want it to last and to keep its scent well, pick the stems just before the tiny flowers open. Bunch, and hang to dry. There are so many things you can do with lavender: add to pot pourri; make 'scent bottles' by folding down the heads and threading ribbon through the stems; make up all-lavender baskets or wreaths; add little bunches or individual flowers to arrangements; and, of course, make your own lavender bags. It prefers a dry, sunny position, but will grow almost anywhere. Clip lavender bushes each spring to keep them from getting untidy, and to encourage new, compact growth with plenty of flowers. The best varieties for colour are 'Hidcote Purple' and 'Twickle Purple'.

Santolina or **cotton lavender** dries quite well. It has tiny little yellow flowers and grey foliage. Pick as for tansy, and clip the bush in the spring to keep it compact and to encourage new growth. Bunch and hang to dry.

If you have room in your garden – for they are both very tall plants – the heads of **angelica** and **elecampane** dry quite well. **Bay leaves** are useful in herb rings for the kitchen, and large heads of **chives** dry, but have to be wired first. The blue heads of **hyssop**, seed heads of **dill**, sprays of **fennel** and the single and double forms of **feverfew** are also worth trying, as is **rosemary**.

The herb garden can provide a range of scented flowers for your dried arrangements.

OTHER PLANTS

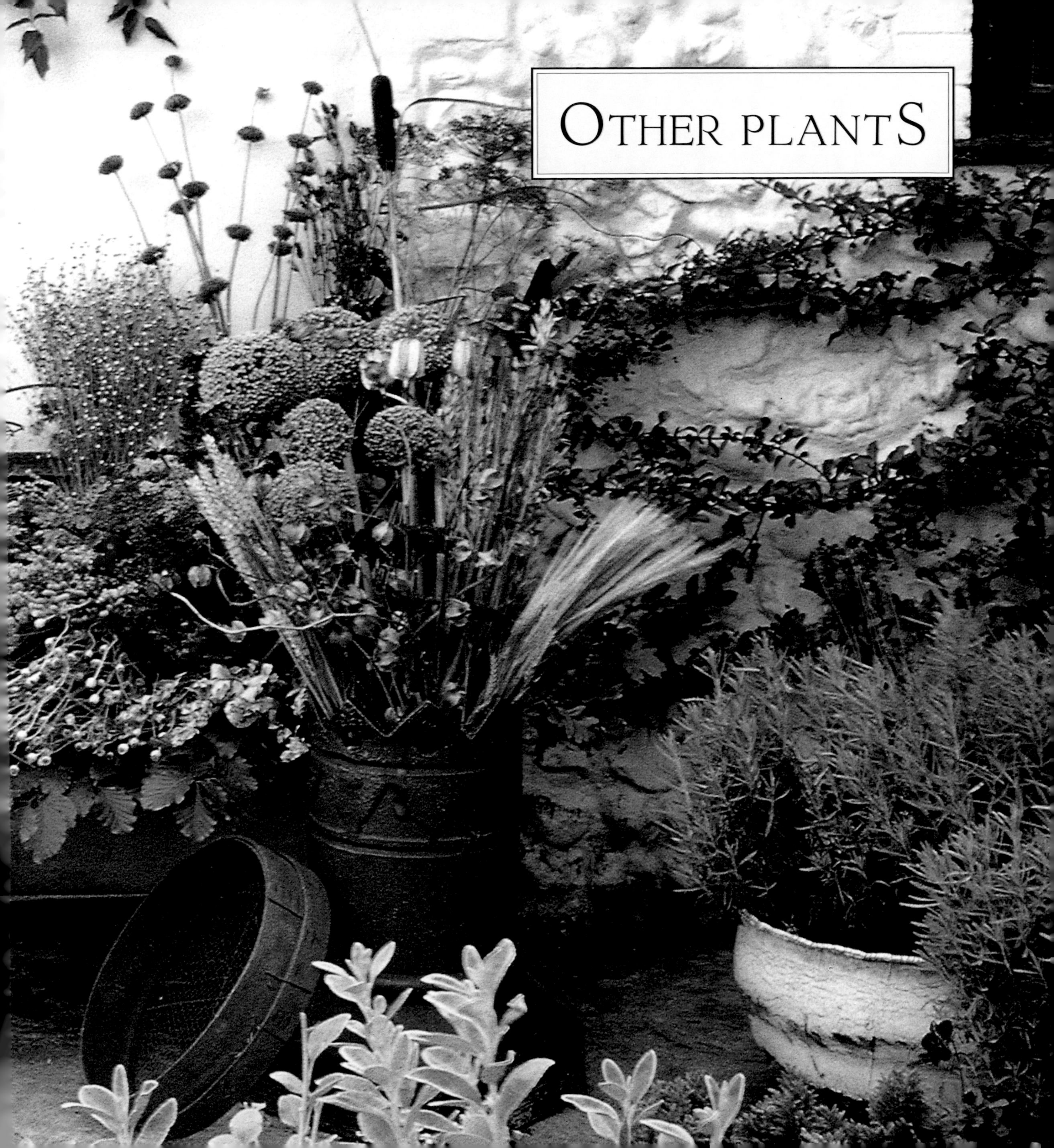

1 *Artemisia ludoviciana;*
2 *Iris foetidissima.*

Although the plants listed here are not really suitable for growing on a large scale, and some do not always dry well, it is worth experimenting with them and, indeed, with any plant you think might dry – you could make a new discovery. For example, pompom dahlias, paeonies and African marigolds all dry quickly over heat.

Artemisia WHITE SAGE

A. ludoviciana (H perennial)
Height: 1–1½ft (30–45cm)
Colour: Silver grey
This plant is slightly invasive, and tends to pop up some distance from where you planted it. However, it is fairly easy to uproot. There are many types of artemisia: some are small shrubs, and some perennials.

How to grow: Very easily! Friends will give you roots, and these will grow almost anywhere in well-drained soil.

Staking: May be necessary if the clump grows very tall.
Pests and diseases: Trouble free.
When to cut: When the leaves are well formed, usually mid- to late summer. You may like to leave picking until the flower stems appear, as these bear silvery-grey buds which can be attractive if not picked too late.
Drying: Strip off a few of the lower leaves, bunch together 8–10 stems and hang to dry. Heat is not necessary, but a warm room is helpful.
Drying time: 1–2 weeks.
Arranging: Useful as outliners and fillers.

Gypsophila BABY'S BREATH

G. elegans (H annual)
Height: 1½–2ft (45–60cm)
Colour: White, pink and red

How to grow: This is the annual variety of gypsophila. It is well worth growing in warm areas. (The perennial variety is better in colder climates.) The flowers are larger than the herbaceous type. Sow outside in spring, and thin out seedlings to 8–10in (20–25cm). This plant likes lime, which should be added if you have acid soil.

Staking: May be necessary if the plants grow tall. Use a twig to prop them up.
Pests and diseases: Usually trouble free.
When to cut: As soon as the heads are well formed.
Drying: Hang together only 1 or 2 stems as they tend to get intertwined.
Drying times: 5–10 days. Some heat is helpful.
Arranging: A pretty finishing touch to all arrangements.

Iris STINKING GLADWYN

I. foetidissima (H perennial)
Height: 1½–2ft (45–60cm)
Colour: Red seeds in a green pod

How to grow: This plant likes moist soil. Friends might give you a piece of rhizome, or it can easily be bought. It dislikes being moved, but as the clumps grow quite large after several years, you will have to lift and divide them. It has insignificant little flowers, and is grown for its seed pods.

Staking: Not necessary.
Pests and diseases: Usually trouble free.
When to cut: When the seed pods are very well formed.
Drying: Take off any leaves; bunch together 6–8 stems and hang to dry in a warm room – not too much heat, or the pods will open too far.

Drying time: 1–2 weeks.
Arranging: Useful in medium and large arrangements. The seeds in the pods do not last more than 2 or 3 months, but are attractive while they keep their colour.

Limonium

L. aureum 'Supernova' and *L. fortunei* 'Confetti'
(HH perennials, but treat as HH annuals)
Height: 1½–2½ft (45–75cm)
Colour: Yellow

How to grow: These are both new introductions, and there is still some confusion over their seeds. 'Confetti' resembles *L. tataricum* (Dumosa); 'Supernova' has larger flowers. In warmer areas they are well worth trying.

Staking: Not necessary.
Pests and diseases: Seem to be trouble free.
When to cut: As soon as the flowers are well formed.
Drying: Bunch 2–3 stems together and hang to dry.
Drying time: 5–10 days.
Arranging: Useful in all arrangements, although 'Confetti' does not keep very well.

PREVIOUS PAGES 118–119:
*A rich harvest of
dried flowers.*

Matricaria GOLD POMPOMS

M. grandiflora, syn. *Chrysanthemum pentzia* (H annual)
Height: 1–1½ft (30–45cm)
Colour: Golden yellow

How to grow: Sow in seed trays, prick out into sectioned trays, harden off and plant out 5–7in (12.5–17.5cm) apart.

Staking: Not necessary.
Pests and diseases: Usually trouble free.
When to cut: As soon as the heads are well formed.
Drying: Remove leaves, bunch 8–10 stems. Hang to dry in a warm room.
Drying time: 8–12 days.
Arranging: Useful in small or medium-sized arrangements.

Salvia CLARY

S. horminum (H annual) S Europe
Height: 1–1½ft (30–45cm)
Colour: All shades

How to grow: Sow outside in spring, and thin out to 5–8in (12.5–20cm). This plant has brightly coloured bracts rather than petals.

Staking: Not necessary.
Pests and diseases: Usually trouble free.
When to cut: When the bracts are well formed and of good colour.
Drying: Bunch together 10–15 stems and hang to dry in a warm room.
Drying time: 5–10 days.
Arranging: Useful in small and medium-sized arrangements.

1 *Salvia horminum;*
2 *Matricaria grandiflora.*

KEY

H perennial =
withstands temperatures
down to 5°F (−15°C)
HH annual =
withstands temperatures
down to 32°F (0°C)
H annual =
withstands temperatures
down to 23°F (−5°C)

1 Hops; **2** *Scabiosa stellata* 'Drumstick'; **3** *Aquilegia*; **4** *Nicandra physaloides*.

Scabiosa SCABIOUS

S. stellata 'Drumstick' (H annual)
Height: 1½–2½ft (45–75cm)
Colour: Seed heads green/beige

How to grow: Sow in seed trays. Prick out into sectioned trays, harden off and plant out 5–8in (12.5–20cm) apart. A sunny position, with well-drained soil is preferable. This plant is grown for its drumstick-shaped seed heads.

Staking: Can be necessary if the plants grow tall.
Pests and diseases: Usually trouble free.
When to cut: When the seed heads are well formed.
Drying: Bunch together 6–8 heads and hang to dry in a warm room.
Drying time: 1–2 weeks.
Arranging: The heads shatter very easily, so care is needed once they are dry. A squirt of hair spray is helpful. Because they are so fragile they are not suitable for growing on a larger scale.

Sedum

S. spectabile × *S. telephium*
Cultivar 'Autumn Joy' (H perennial)
Height: 1½–2ft (45–60cm)
Colour: Pink shading to orange/red

How to grow: Very easily. Friends may be able to give you a small clump, which will soon establish itself.

Staking: No.
Pests and diseases: Trouble free.
When to cut: When the heads are well formed and of good colour.

Drying: Bunch together 3–5 stems and hang to dry in a warm room.
Drying time: 1–2 weeks.
Arranging: The heads of this plant dry reasonably well, but do not remain in good condition for more than a few months. Useful in medium-sized to large arrangements.

Seed Heads and Pods

Poppy seed pods are listed in the Plant Directory, but other plants produce heads that can be used, too. **Tulips**, for example, produce good pods, which should be removed for the good of the bulb. The spring variety 'Tarda' has excellent pods – pick these before they open, otherwise they seed everywhere. Hang up to dry, and shake out the seeds. They can be sprayed gold.

Cultivated **hops** are charming, but be sure to ask before helping yourself to these. Small cobs of **sweetcorn** can be attractive in large arrangements when dried, with the leaves gently stripped back from the cob.

Paeony, aquilegia and the seed heads of **montbretia, leeks, decorative alliums** and **onions** are worth trying, as are the balloon-shaped pods of *Nicandra physaloides*, and the tiny heads of **sisyrinchium**.

The seed heads of **foxglove** and **verbascum** sometimes dry well in a good summer; pick before they start turning brown or are spoiled by bad weather. **Phlomis** (Jerusalem sage) can also be picked when green, and sometimes dries successfully.

Roses

Very few roses hang dry well, and most will have to be dried using borax or silica gel crystals. However, the tiny tight-headed roses that can be bought from florists respond quite successfully to being dried quickly over heat. Care is needed when handling them once they are dry, as they become brittle.

Drying time will be from one to two weeks, depending on the size of the heads, and how much heat you give them. Old-fashioned roses such as 'Madame Isaac Pereire' or 'The Fairy' are best to experiment with. A great deal depends on when you pick the rose; a too-tight bud or an overblown bloom will not air dry well. The floribunda 'Ann Crocker' dries well in borax.

Beyond the Garden Wall

There is a wealth of material available beyond the garden wall. But remember that many wild flowers are protected, and on no account must the seed heads of these be taken, for they need to be left to self-sow for the following year. Also, be sure to ask your local farmer before you help yourself to any of his wheat, oats or barley.

In addition to wild flowers, many **wild grasses** such as timothy grass, crow's foot grass and even couch grass dry well and are useful. Pick them early, while they are still green; bunch them and hang them up to dry. Several types of reed grass, found in or near ponds, dry well too. **Bulrushes** are marvellous for large arrangements. You will need to give the heads a squirt of hair spray once they are dry to prevent them bursting open in the warmth of your house. **Fir cones** can be found in all shapes and sizes, and can be used either as they are or sprayed gold.

Through the garden gate.

123

APPENDICES

Seed Quantities

ANNUALS

The quantity of seed in packets varies between suppliers. Order early to avoid out-of-stock returns, and to allow time to send for extra packets if necessary.

Plant Name	Seed Packets	
	OWN USE	LARGER SCALE
Amaranthus (each colour)	1	1–3
Ammobium	1	1–2
Carthamus	1	3–4
Centaurea	1	1–2
Craspedia	1	3–4
Delphinium (Larkspur) (each colour)	1	2–4
Gomphrena	1	2–3
Helichrysum		
H. bracteatum 'Bikini' (each colour)	1	1–2
H. bracteatum 'Monstrosum' (each colour)	1	1–2
H. cassinianum	1	3–4
H. subulifolium	1	1–3
Helipterum		
H. humboldtianum	1	1–3
H. manglesii	1	2–3

Plant Name	Seed Packets	
	OWN USE	LARGER SCALE
H. roseum (each colour)	1	2–3
H. splendidum	2	3–6
Limonium		
L. sinuatum (each colour)	1	2–4
L. suworowii	1	1–2
Linum	1	1–3
Lonas	1	1–3
Moluccella	1	2–4
Nigella	1	2–3
Papaver	1	1–3
Xeranthemum	1	3–4

GRASSES

Quantities of grass seed vary greatly between suppliers.

Plant Name	Seed Packets	
	OWN USE	LARGER SCALE
Briza		
B. maxima	1	1–2
B. minor	1	1–2
Lagurus	1	3–6
Phalaris	1	2–5
Setaria		
S. glauca	1	1–2
S. macrochaeta	1	2–5
Triticum	2–3	4–8

Plant Quantities

ANNUALS

These quantities are only a guide. After your first season you will have a better idea of how many plants you require.

Plant Name	OWN USE	LARGER SCALE (ROWS)
Plants		
Amaranthus (each colour)	5–10	1 × 15–25ft (4.5–7.5m)
Ammobium	10–20	1 × 15–25ft (4.5–7.5m) (double row)
Carthamus	4–8	1 × 15–25ft (4.5–7.5m)
Centaurea	5–10	1 × 10–15ft (3–4.5m) (double row)
Craspedia	6–10	1 × 15–25ft (4.5–7.5m)
Delphinum (Larkspur) (each colour)	4–8	1 × 15–25ft (4.5–7.5m)
Gomphrena	6–10	1 × 15–25ft (4.5–7.5m)
Helichrysum		
H. bracteatum 'Bikini' (each colour)	3–5	1 × 15–25ft (4.5–7.5m)
H. bracteatum 'Monstrosum' (each colour)	3–5	1 × 15–25ft (4.5–7.5m)
H. cassinianum	3–6	1 × 10–20ft (3–6m)
H. subulifolium	4–8	2 × 15–25ft (4.5–7.5m)
Helipterum		
H. humboldtianum	6–10	1 × 15–25ft (4.5–7.5m)
H. manglesii	4–8	1 × 15–25ft (4.5–7.5m)
H. roseum	5–15	1 × 15–20ft (4.5–6m)
H. splendidum	6–20	1 × 15–25ft (4.5–7.5m)
Limonium		
L. sinuatum (each colour)	4–8	1 × 15–25ft (4.5–7.5m)

Plant Name	OWN USE	LARGER SCALE (ROWS)
Plants		
L. suworowii	6–10	2 × 15–25ft (4.5–7.5m)
Linum	4–8	1 × 15–25ft (4.5–7.5m)
Lonas	4–8	1 × 10–15ft (3–4.5m)
Moluccella	5–10	1 × 15–25ft (4.5–7.5m)
Nigella	8–12	1 × 20–25ft (6–7.5m)
Papaver	4–8	1 × 15–25ft (4.5–7.5m)
Xeranthemum	6–10	1 × 15–20ft (4.5–6m) (double row)

PERENNIALS

These quantities are based on well established plants, and are only a guide.

Acanthus, artichokes and teasels are all very large plants, and it is better to place these in a part of the garden where they are easily managed and do not get in the way of other rows or individual clumps.

Stachys lanata tends to wander about, and is better placed where it can do this without spreading into other plants.

Physalis can become invasive, so is best planted well away from your clumps or rows of flowers, in an area where its wayward habit can be controlled.

Plant Name	OWN USE	LARGER SCALE (ROWS)
Plants		
Acanthus	1–3	1 × 10–15ft (3–4.5m)
Achillea	2–4	1 × 10–20ft (3–6m)
Alchemilla	2–4	1 × 15–20ft (4.5–6m)
Anaphalis	1–2	1 × 10–15ft (3–4.5m)
Artichoke	1–3	1 × 10–15ft (3–4.5m)

Plant Name	Plants		Plant Name	Plants	
	OWN USE	LARGER SCALE (ROWS)		OWN USE	LARGER SCALE (ROWS)
Astilbe (each colour)	1–3	1 × 10–15ft (3–4.5m)	Solidago	2–4	1 × 15–25ft (4.5–7.5m)
Astrantia	1–3	1 × 10–15ft (3–4.5m)	Stachys	3–6	1 × 10–15ft (3–4.5m)'
Carlina	3–5	1 × 15–25ft (4.5–7.5m)			
Catananche	1–2	1 × 4–8ft (1.2–2.4m)			

GRASSES

Plant Name	Plants	
	OWN USE	LARGER SCALE (ROWS)

Plant Name	Plants		Plant Name	Plants	
	OWN USE	LARGER SCALE (ROWS)		OWN USE	LARGER SCALE (ROWS)
Centaurea	2–4	1 × 15–25ft (4.5–7.5m)	Briza		
Cirsium	2–4	1 × 15–20ft (4.5–6m)	B. maxima	1 × 3–5ft (1–1.5m)	1 × 15–20ft (4.5–6m)
Delphinium	3–5	1 × 15–25ft (4.5–7.5m)	B. minor	1 × 3–5ft (1–1.5m)	1 × 15–20ft (4.5–6m)
Dipsacus	1–3	1 × 10–15ft (3–4.5m)	Lagurus	1 × 3–5ft (1–1.5m)	1 × 15–25ft (4.5–7.5m)
Echinops			Phalaris	1 × 4–6ft (1.2–1.8m)	1 × 15–25ft (4.5–7.5m)
E. ritro	1–2	1 × 15–20ft (4.5–6m)			
E. sphaerocephalus	2–4	1 × 15–25ft (4.5–7.5m)	Setaria		
Eryngium (each variety)	2–4	1 × 15–25ft (4.5–7.5m)	S. glauca	1 × 4–6ft (1.2–1.8m)	1 × 25ft (7.5m)
Gnaphalium	2–4	1 × 10–15ft (3–4.5m)	S. macro-chaeta	1 × 5–8ft (1.5–2.4m)	2 × 25ft (7.5m)
Gypsophila	1–2	1 × 10–15ft (3–4.5m)	Triticum	1 × 6–8ft (1.8–2.4m)	1 × 25ft (7.5m)
Helichrysum					
H. acuminatum	2–4	1 × 10–15ft (3–4.5m)			
Hydrangea	1–2	4–6 bushes			
Liatris	2–4	1 × 10–20ft (3–6m)			
Limonium	6–8	1 × 15–25ft (4.5–7.5m)			
Linum	2–4	1 × 10–15ft (3–4.5m)			
Lunaria	2–4	1 × 15–25ft (4.5–7.5m)			
Physalis	4–8	1 × 15–25ft (4.5–7.5m)			
Polygonum	1–2	1 × 10–15ft (3–4.5m)			

INDEX